English Code 6

Activity Book

Contents

OUR WORLD

INTRO:

Here we stand: children of every age,
This is our world and the world's our stage.
We can laugh, we can cry — we can float, we can fly,
We can dance, we can sing — we can do almost anything
in OUR world ... our *beautiful* world.

VERSE 1:

Some of us are small; some of us are tall,
Some of us are shy; some say hi to everybody,
Some of us like numbers; some of us love words,
Some of us watch football, and some of us watch the birds!

(CHORUS)

This is *our* world ... we're different but the same.
We live and learn together — we get to know each other ...
in OUR world ... our *beautiful* world.

VERSE 2:

Some of us like music; some of us like cars,
Some of us draw pictures, looking at the stars,
Some of us are scientists, trying to find the code,
All of us can help a friend and give a hand to hold.

This is *our* world — there's room for everyone.
We learn to live together, and we have a lot of fun ...
In **our** world ... in **our** world ... in our beautiful world!

Progress Chart

Unit 8

Unit 7

Unit 6

Unit 5

Unit 4

Unit 3

Unit 2

Unit 1

Creativity

Collaboration

4

Critical Thinking

Coding

Communication

Welcome!

> How can I talk about my school timetable?

1 Read and complete.

2 _____ is over. I must put my packed lunch in my 3 _____ .

Let's see what lesson is next on my 1 _____ .

See you in class!

2 🎧 002 Listen and complete.

MONDAY
8:50
9:55
11:00
11:20
12:25
1:30
2:20
3:30

3 🎧 002 Listen again and answer the questions.

1 Where are the lockers?

_____

2 What time does break start?

_____

3 What time is lunch?

_____

4 What is the Art teacher like?

_____

4 Can you work out which letters open the locker?

CODE CRACKER ⚙️⚙️⚙️

C D B – none of the letters are correct

B G C – none of the letters are correct

A F E – two letters are correct, but only one letter is in the correct order

H E C – two letters are correct, but only one letter is in the correct order

H F E – two letters are correct, but they are in the wrong order

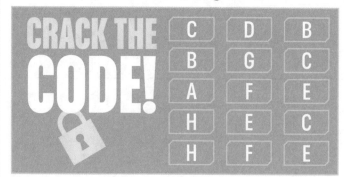

CRACK THE CODE!

C	D	B
B	G	C
A	F	E
H	E	C
H	F	E

The school day

VOCABULARY

I will learn words to talk about the school day.

1 Read and complete.

> assembly   bell rings   break   canteen   corridor
> detention   gym   locker   packed lunch
> portable classrooms   queue   timetable

Date: 27th September

Today is the first day of the new term! We've got our 1 _____ , so we can see
what subjects we've got every day. Before school starts, I usually meet my friends in the
2 _____ where we can chat and talk about our homework from the day before.
On Monday morning, the whole school meets for an 3 _____ . So when the
4 _____ at 8:50 a.m., we all 5 _____ and then walk into
the school 6 _____ . It's really big so we use it for PE, too.

We've got three lessons in the morning, and then there's a 20-minute 7 _____ .
Our school is growing! We've got two new 8 _____ on the other
side of the playground this term – one is for English, and one is for History. Lunch is in the
9 _____ at 12:45 p.m. I usually go to my 10 _____ – lucky number five! –
to get my 11 _____ , and then I have my lunch while I chat with
my friends. In the afternoon, we've got PE. Students who don't do their homework can't
go to PE. They have to go to the library for 12 _____ . That usually means extra
homework …!

2 Work it out!

MATHS ZONE

Half of the pieces of fruit in these
children's packed lunches are apples.
There are three oranges, two pears
and one banana. How many apples
are there in the packed lunches?

3 Design a locker label. Choose
some decorations to stick on it.

I can use words to talk about the school day.

Language lab

GRAMMAR: *LIKE*

1 🔧 Read the questions and answers below. Are they about personality (P), likes and dislikes (L) or appearance (A)?

1 What does he/she look like? ____

2 He/She likes sport and books. ____

3 He/She is very friendly. ____

4 What is he/she like? ____

5 What does he/she like? ____

6 He/She has got long hair and glasses. ____

2 Think of a person who you know. Answer the questions in 1.

1 _____

4 _____

5 _____

3 💬 Work with a partner. Ask and answer the questions in 1 to find out about the person in 2.

What does he look like?

He's tall, he's got curly hair and he wears glasses.

Values Be welcoming.

4 What is more important: what a person is like, what a person looks like or what a person likes? Discuss with a partner.

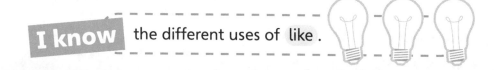

I know the different uses of **like**.

Story lab

READING

The Wrong Riley

1 💡 **Look at the words and expressions from *The Wrong Riley*. Use the context of the story or a dictionary to help you work out the meanings.**

> catch my eye   clutch   confused   double   lie   turn upside down   yell

2 💡 **Choose three of the words and expressions from 1. Write a definition of each in your own words. Then tell your definitions to a partner. Can they guess the word or expression?**

1 _____

2 _____

3 _____

3 **Find and underline the incorrect information in each sentence. Write the correct information.**

1 Riley is feeling a little excited before the first day of term at his new school.   _____

2 Riley's Welcome Buddy seems really shy.   _____

3 Samira has got long, curly hair and glasses.   _____

4 Riley wants to give his Welcome Buddy a Maths book.   _____

4 ⚙️ **Imagine *The Wrong Riley* is a film. Follow the steps below and draw a film poster.**

- Go online to find other film posters to give you ideas for your poster.

- Think about which actors are in the film.

- Make your poster as colourful, exciting and imaginative as possible.

The Wrong Riley

5 💬 **Present your poster to the class. Have a class vote to find out which poster is the best.**

I can read a comedy story.

In the news

How can I make a video news report?

1 Read and complete.

1 A _____ writes news.

2 A _____ is a sentence that describes a photo.

3 The _____ tells us what a news story is about.

4 Did you read the interesting _____ in yesterday's newspaper?

2 Listen. How do these people follow the news? Tick ☑ the things they mention.

	Newspaper	Online news	Websites	TV	Radio
Bobbie					
Vanessa					
Ollie					

3 How do you follow the news? Ask and answer in pairs.

4 Read the article. Who was the thief?

CODE CRACKER

LOCAL NEWS   **2ND FEBRUARY**

BURGLARY AT THE JEWELLERY SHOP

Last night there was a burglary at a jewellery shop in town. The police spoke to three people: Mr Gold, Miss Diamond and Mr Silver. The police knew that one of them was the thief and that only one of them told the truth.

Miss Diamond said, 'I am not the thief.'

Mr Gold said, 'Miss Diamond is the thief.'

Mr Silver said, 'I am not the thief.'

Social media club

VOCABULARY

I will learn words to talk about social media and news.

1 Read and match.

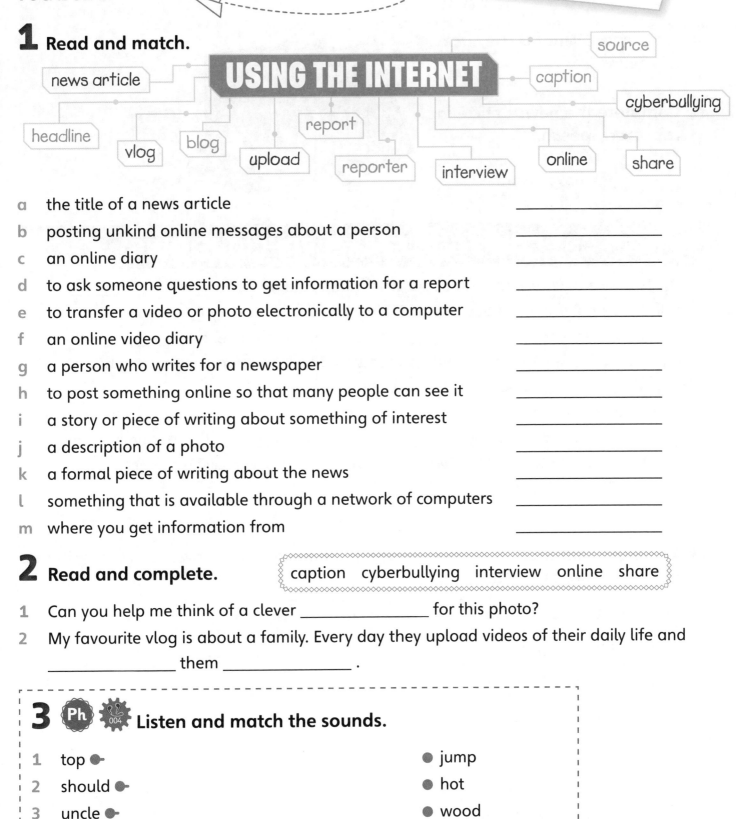

USING THE INTERNET

source
caption
cyberbullying
news article
headline
report
vlog
blog
upload
reporter
interview
online
share

a   the title of a news article _____

b   posting unkind online messages about a person _____

c   an online diary _____

d   to ask someone questions to get information for a report _____

e   to transfer a video or photo electronically to a computer _____

f   an online video diary _____

g   a person who writes for a newspaper _____

h   to post something online so that many people can see it _____

i   a story or piece of writing about something of interest _____

j   a description of a photo _____

k   a formal piece of writing about the news _____

l   something that is available through a network of computers _____

m   where you get information from _____

2 Read and complete.

caption   cyberbullying   interview   online   share

1   Can you help me think of a clever _____ for this photo?

2   My favourite vlog is about a family. Every day they upload videos of their daily life and _____ them _____ .

3 Ph 004 Listen and match the sounds.

1   top ●   ● jump
2   should ●   ● hot
3   uncle ●   ● wood

I can use words to talk about social media and news.

Language lab

GRAMMAR 1: REPORTED SPEECH

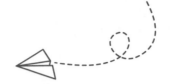
I will learn to use reported speech.

1  Listen. What is the *Lucky dip* game?

2 Complete the news article in reported speech.

> be   have   want

SCHOOLBOY FINDS POP STAR'S PRECIOUS RING | 1st May

We spoke to Patrick Jackson about what happened. He said that it **1** _____ his school Bring and Buy sale on Friday. The pop star, Missy P, was coming to give prizes. Patrick said he **2** _____ an idea for a fun game. It **3** _____ the Lucky Dip game. The kids all brought presents to school and put them in a big box. There **4** _____ some great presents. Patrick said he **5** _____ to get the leather wallet. On the day of the sale, Missy P discovered that her diamond ring was missing. She was very unhappy, but she said perhaps it **6** _____ at home. When it was Patrick's turn to take a mystery prize out of the box, he picked up a beautiful ring. It was Missy P's ring!

3 Write the sentences in reported speech. Then read the news article again and circle T (True) or F (False).

1 We can all bring prizes to school to put in the Lucky Dip box.   T / F

Patrick said _____ .

2 I want to get the card game.   T / F

Patrick said _____ .

3 My ring is at home.   T / F

Missy P said _____ .

4 I don't know whose ring it is.   T / F

Missy P said _____ .

4 Can you guess the pattern on the Lucky Numbers game?

MATHS ZONE

Guess the missing numbers!

8	16	24	32	40	48
3	6	9	12	15	18
12	24	⭐ ____	48	⭐ ____	72

5 Write the sentences in reported speech.

1 **The children:** 'We've all got prizes to put in the Lucky Dip box.'

_____

_____

_____

2 **Missy P:** 'My ring is missing. I don't know where it is.'

_____

_____

_____

3 **Patrick:** 'I want to try and guess the missing numbers.'

_____

_____

4 **Joe:** 'I'm not usually very good at number games. I find Maths difficult.'

_____

_____

5 **Miriam:** 'I look for patterns, for example, all even numbers or all multiples of five.'

_____

_____

6 Think and discuss. What can your school do to collect money for new projects?

7 What do you do to help people? Make sentences in the Present Simple. Next, work in pairs and tell your partner your sentences. Then form new pairs. Can you remember what your first partner said?

Cameron said he always gave his old books and toys to younger students at school.

 I can use reported speech.

Story lab

I will read a mystery story.

The mystery of the missing necklace

1 💡 Number the events in the correct order.

a ☐ Annisa started writing her report.

b ☐ Annisa went to Mr Budi's shop.

c ☐ There was a burglary.

d ☐ The police spoke to people in the shop.

e ☐ Annisa had breakfast.

f ☐ The police spoke to Annisa.

g ☐ Annisa wanted to speak to Mr Budi.

2 Read and circle the correct answer.

1 When did Annisa hear about the burglary?

  a when she went to the centre of town on her bike

  b while she was having breakfast

  c when she was listening to the radio in bed

2 What kind of shop did Mr Budi have?

  a a jewellery shop

  b a school stationery shop

  c a gift shop

3 Where did Annisa live?

  a in the centre of the town

  b at the top of a hill

  c at the bottom of a hill

4 Who was interviewing people about the burglary?

  a Annisa

  b Mr Budi

  c the police officer

5 How did people describe the thief?

  a short, black hair and big feet

  b long, black hair and small feet

  c short, black hair and small feet

6 What did the police tell Annisa to do?

  a not to try and help them

  b not to talk to Mr Budi

  c not to be in the shop

7 Why did Annisa decide to talk to Mr Budi?

  a because she felt sorry for him

  b to ask him what he thought

  c to ask him to describe the necklace

8 Why did Annisa say, 'I think I've got my story!'?

  a because she knew the thief was a monkey

  b because she wanted to interview Mr Budi

  c because she had an idea for a story about a monkey

3 Find words in the story that mean ...

1   ... lost, gone, misplaced. _____

2   ... very special, unusual and expensive. _____

3   ... someone who takes something that belongs to someone else. _____

4   ... very well-known. _____

5   ... marks that are made by shoes or feet. _____

6   ... tips, signs, signals, suggestions. _____

4   Listen and find three mistakes in the radio news report.

_____

_____

_____

5   These sentences are missing from the story. Who said them? Write them in reported speech.

1   [I have to go out, Mum. I've got an important errand to run.]

_____

2   [We are good at finding out information about burglaries!]

_____

3   [Hi, Mr Budi! I'm very sorry about your necklace.]

_____

6   Think about the story. What do you think happened next? Write the next paragraph in your notebook.

TOWN NEWS

THE MYSTERY OF THE MISSING NECKLACE

The next day, ...

_____

_____

7   Make a reporter's notebook.

Notebook

I can read a mystery story.

I will learn about different states of water.

1 Complete the crossword.

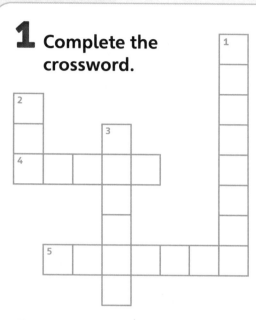

Down

1 0 degrees Celsius is _____ point.

2 Water vapour is a _____ .

3 Water is a _____ .

Across

4 Ice is a _____ .

5 100 degrees Celsius is the _____ point of water.

2 Read and complete. Then match.

crash   dense   expands   hexagonal   molecules   spread   steam

THE CHANGING STATES OF WATER

1 ☐ When water is a liquid, the _____ move around all the time. They _____ into each other and move over and under each other.

2 ☐ When water is a gas – also called water vapour or _____ – the molecules can move past each other more easily. They _____ out in all directions.

3 ☐ When water freezes and becomes a solid, the molecules start to move more slowly, until finally they stop moving. They become _____ rings, and when it gets even colder, these rings become snowflakes. As water freezes, it _____ and takes up more space. It also becomes less _____ , in other words, less heavy than water.

a

b

c

3 Write S (Solid), L (Liquid) or G (Gas).

1. ☐
2. ☐
3. ☐
4. ☐
5. ☐
6. ☐

4 Choose one of the pictures from **3** and draw the molecule pattern.

EXPERIMENT TIME

Report

1 Draw the results of your experiment in cups a, b and c.

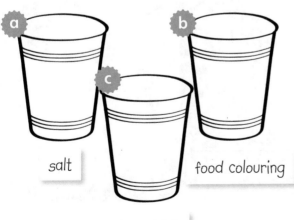

a

b

c

salt

food colouring

fizzy drink

2 Write your report.

Freezing different materials

When you freeze salt water, the ice is cloudy.

(Salt water) _____

(Food colouring) _____

(Fizzy drink) _____

I know about different states of water.

He asked me if ...

COMMUNICATION: REPORTED SPEECH QUESTIONS

I will learn about reporting an interview.

1 Write questions in the Present Simple to find out general and personal information about someone. Use the ideas below or your own ideas.

> age   appearance   family   hobbies and interests   name
> nationality   school   sport   subjects   town or city

Do _____ ?   When _____ ?

Who _____ ?   Why _____ ?

What _____ ?   How often _____ ?

Where _____ ?   How old _____ ?

2 Choose three questions from 1. Ask and answer with a partner.

When do you get up in the morning?

I get up at half past seven.

3 Write your partner's answers, using reported speech. Read your sentences to your partner. Did you write the information correctly?

She said she gets up at seven.

4 Play the *Telephone game*.

I can report an interview.

Writing lab

I will write a podcast.

WRITING A PODCAST

1 Read and match.

HOME   VIDEOS   BOOKS   SHOP

SPEAKER	TEXT
Presenter:	Milly Franklin was walking on the beach with her dog last weekend when she heard a man shouting for help. Milly, tell us what happened next.
Milly:	Well, I couldn't see anyone. But then my dog ran towards the rocks. I followed him. And that's when we saw the man. He was lying on the sand and there was a rock on his leg. He couldn't get free. I'm sure it was very painful.
Presenter:	What did you do?
Milly:	I tried to pull the rock off his leg, but it was very heavy. Luckily, I had my phone with me. I phoned the emergency services, and they came very quickly.
Presenter:	Is the man OK? How did it happen?
Milly:	Yes, he was lucky. They took him to hospital. He's only got a broken leg. He was fishing when he slipped, and the rock rolled on top of his leg.
Presenter:	I'm sure he's very happy you came along at the right time!

1 Who found the man? •
2 What did the dog do? •
3 When did it happen? •

● last weekend
● Milly and her dog
● He ran to the rocks.

2 🔩 Find and underline three facts and three opinions in the script.

3 🔩 Use the diagram to help you plan a podcast script. Write notes about each question word in your notebook.

4 🚀 Write a podcast script. Include at least three facts and three opinions.

why   who   ?   what   when   where

I can write a podcast.

Make a video news report

1 Compare a news report with a podcast script. What is the same or different?

	A video news report	A podcast script
Who tells the story?		
How do you find out what the story is about?		
What visuals are there?		
Which one has more examples of reported speech?		

2 Write your project report.

- Our report is about:

  _____

- We used the following sources to find information:

  _____

- Examples of visuals in our report include:

  _____

- We used the following examples of reported speech:

  _____

3 Present your report to your family and friends.

I can make a video news report.

1 Match the pieces to make words from the unit.

2 Write the questions and answers in reported speech.

What time do you get up?

At half past four!

How do you get here every morning?

I get a taxi because there aren't any buses at that time in the morning.

How do you like to spend your free time?

I sleep!

1 I asked her _____ .

2 She _____ .

3 I asked her _____ .

4 She _____ .

5 I asked her _____ .

6 She _____ .

3  Work in pairs. Ask and answer the questions in 2. Then tell the class something your partner said.

She said she likes listening to music in her free time.

Now go to your Progress Chart on page 4.

2 Inspirational people

How can I make a book about inspirational people?

1 Read and write.

> brave   compassionate   inspirational   intelligent   kind

1   inspires people to do good things or be creative _____

2   understands how people and animals are feeling _____

3   unafraid to do difficult things _____

4   friendly, generous and likes to help other people _____

5   clever _____

2 Listen to the conversation about jobs. What characteristics do you need for each job?

Job	Characteristics

3 Look at the Venn diagram. What do the letters B, C and I mean? Why is the letter C in the middle section?

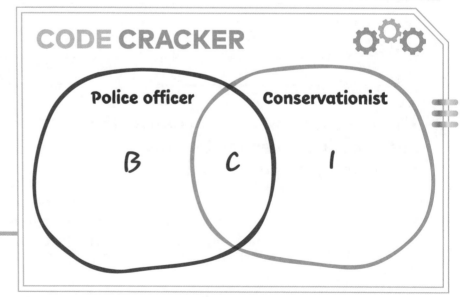

CODE CRACKER

Police officer   Conservationist

B   C   I

Inspirational people

VOCABULARY

I will learn words to describe people and their jobs.

1 Which words are nouns and which are adjectives? Write *n* or *adj*.

1 author _____   2 brave _____   3 campaigner _____   4 charity worker _____

5 compassionate _____   6 determined _____   7 generous _____   8 inspirational _____

9 intelligent _____   10 lawyer _____   11 researcher _____   12 volunteer _____

2 Unscramble the words and complete the email.

roauht   nrecgpmaai   cmpssnteaoiao   eieerddnmt   osprtnlniiiaa   entgnieillt

Hi Jack,

I just had a conversation with an **1** _____ lawyer. She works to help people in poor countries. She inspires a lot of people with the work she does. She is also a **2** _____ for human rights. She wants everybody in the world to be equal. She's also an **3** _____ . She's written a lot of books about the work she does around the world. I asked her what characteristics you need to be a successful lawyer. She told me that you need to be **4** _____ because you need to help people in trouble and you need to be **5** _____ . This is because when you make a decision to do something, you can't change your mind! Oh, and one more thing. She said that it helps if you are **6** _____ .
You need to study a lot to become a lawyer!

Olivia

EXTRA VOCABULARY

3 Read and complete. Use a dictionary to help you.

Adjective	Noun
1 brave	_____
2 compassionate	_____
3 generous	_____
4 inspirational	_____

4 (Ph) (008) Listen. Then say the tongue twister as quickly as you can.

He eats bread for breakfast and has peas with tea.

She dreams of heavy feathers when she reads of healthy weather.

I can use words to describe people and their jobs.

Language lab

GRAMMAR 1: RELATIVE CLAUSES

I will learn to use relative clauses.

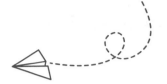

1 Read and circle.

1 A volunteer is someone who / **whose** agrees to work for no money.

2 Do you know the city **where** / which the campaign started?

3 I know someone who / **whose** father is a researcher.

4 The charity worker decided to act when / **that** she saw the terrible news.

5 This is the book that / **who** was written by the famous lawyer.

2 Complete with relative pronouns and match.

1 A hospital is a place _____ •   • is brave and compassionate.

2 A police officer is someone _____ •   • helps you to find your way.

3 This is my friend _____ •   • we don't go to school.

4 A compass is something _____ •   • a nurse works.

5 Summer is a time _____ •   • parents work in a foreign country.

3 🎧 009 Listen to the definitions and complete the sentences. What words are being described?

1 This is a word _____ describes someone _____ isn't _____ to do something. _____

2 This is a website _____ you can read online what people _____ . _____

3 This is a person _____ job is to understand _____ . _____

4 This is _____ you put music, videos or photographs on a _____ . _____

5 This is a person _____ writes _____ . _____

4 Think of three words and write a definition using relative pronouns. Read your definitions to the class. Can they guess the words?

_____

_____

_____

5 Join the sentences with relative clauses and pronouns.

1   Greta Thunberg is an inspirational young person.
    She is an environmental campaigner.

    _____

2   She started to learn about the environment and climate
    change. She was eight years old.

    _____

3   She was so upset at what was happening to the planet she
    stopped speaking. She was 11.

    _____

4   Greta went to the Swedish parliament. She started to protest against climate change
    every Friday.

    _____

5   News of Greta spread on social media. This resulted in many young people protesting
    against climate change every Friday.

    _____

6 Make sentences using the phrases below or your own ideas. Tell your sentences to a partner.

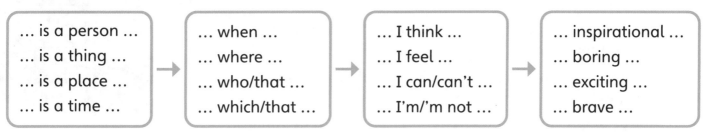

… is a person …	… when …	… I think …	… inspirational …
… is a thing …	… where …	… I feel …	… boring …
… is a place …	… who/that …	… I can/can't …	… exciting …
… is a time …	… which/that …	… I'm/'m not …	… brave …

My dad is a person who I think is inspirational.

Winter is a time when I feel cold.

I can use relative clauses.

25

Story lab

I will read a biographical story.

THE HUGGING LION

1 Read and match,

1   orphaned •   • a young big cat
2   free •   • area of grassland in Africa
3   cub •   • when a baby has no parents
4   plains •   • a person or thing that brings good luck to a company or event
5   mascot •   • not in captivity
6   paws •   • the feet of a big cat

2 Read and circle T (True) or F (False). Correct the false sentences.

1   Joy and George Adamson worked as conservationists
    and campaigners.   T / F

2   George Adamson was famous for writing a book called
    Born Free.   T / F

3   A shop in London sold a lion cub to two people called
    John and Joy.   T / F

4   John and Ace often took Chris, the lion cub, to cafés
    in London.   T / F

5   Chris's owners thought it was wrong to take him to Kenya.   T / F

6   Many people have seen a video of Chris and his old owners. T / F

_____

_____

_____

3 Read and complete.

1   The Adamsons were animal conservationists and _____ who lived in
    Kenya, Africa.

2   Elsa was a lion cub whose mother was _____ .

3   Joy Adamson was _____ towards lions.

4 Read the interview with John, who was one of Chris's owners. Write the questions.

1 _____

I first saw Chris when I went into a department store in London with my friend Ace.

2 _____

I felt really surprised when I saw Chris for sale.

3 _____

We took Chris out for walks every day and often took him to the beach.

4 _____

Ace and I decided to take Chris to Kenya.

5 _____

We felt happy when we saw Chris again, but we were nervous because he was now an adult lion.

5 Use your own ideas to answer the questions.

1 Who shot the lion cub's mother?
2 How did Joy Adamson feel when she set Elsa free?
3 How did people react when they saw Chris, the lion cub, out for walks in London?
4 Why was it the best thing for John and Ace to take Chris to Kenya?
5 How do you think people react when they see the video of Chris with his former owners?

6 What is your favourite part of the story and why? Draw a picture of it in your notebook and tell a partner about it.

Values Value yourself.

7 Look at the qualities that the people in the story have. Do you have some of these qualities? What other qualities do you have? Tell a partner about a time you cared for an animal (or a person). What did you do? How did it make you feel?

I can read a biographical story.

Experiment lab

I will learn about mould and bacteria.

1 Read and complete.

bacteria   microscope   mould   particle   slide

1 Some people believe that all _____ are bad for us, but there are some which live in our stomach to keep us healthy.

2 A _____ is a very small piece of something.

3 Scientists use an instrument called a _____ to be able to see very small things.

4 _____ is something which grows in very damp conditions.

5 She placed the mould particles on a _____ and looked at them under a microscope.

2 Read and answer.

1 Why does the author of the text think Dr Alexander Fleming is an inspirational person?

_____

2 How did Dr Fleming discover that mould killed bacteria?

_____

3 Read and answer.

MATHS ZONE

How big are bacteria?

Bacteria are very, very small. We don't use millimetres, centimetres or metres to measure how big bacteria are. We use a unit of measurement called a micrometre. There are 1000 micrometres to every millimetre. Look at how big some bacteria are:

- E. coli – 2 micrometres long
- streptococcus pneumoniae – 1.25 micrometres long
- borrelia – 3 micrometres long

1 How many E. coli bacteria can fit in one millimetre? __1000 ÷ 2 = 500__

2 How many E. coli bacteria can fit in two millimetres? _____

3 How many streptococcus pneumoniae bacteria can fit in two millimetres?

_____

4 How many borrelia bacteria can fit in three millimetres? _____

4 **Read the leaflet. What types of mould does it mention?**

Fun facts about mould!

- Mould comes in many different colours. It can be black, green, pink, yellow, red, brown and blue.

- Many of us happily eat mould. It's true! As well as in medicine, we also use penicillin in the production of some types of cheese, like brie from France.

- Fungi is another type of mould and you see this every time you go food shopping. Mushrooms are fungi. So are truffles, which we also eat. Did you know that someone once paid £330,000 for one single truffle?

- Not all mould is good for us. Some types are very bad for our health. We shouldn't eat some fungi, and if you see mould growing on your food, don't put it in your mouth. That's because this mould is very poisonous.

- Some mould actually moves around. Slime mould can move about 200 metres every hour. Imagine that following you home at night!

EXPERIMENT TIME

Report

1 **Think about your experiment. Use green to colour the bread with the most mould.**

Damp bread

fridge   room temperature   warm place

Dry bread

fridge   room temperature   warm place

2 **Answer the questions.**

1 How should we store bread if we want to keep it free from mould?

2 What other food do you think will grow mould if it is kept in a warm, damp place?

3 **Think about your experiment. Discuss with a partner.**

- What worked?
- What went wrong?
- What will you do differently next time?

I know about mould and bacteria.

Being different!

COMMUNICATION: *USED TO*

I will learn how to talk about past habits and states.

1 Listen to an interview with David and tick ☑ .

1 Did David use to play tennis when he was eight years old?

Yes, he did. ☐   No, he didn't. ☐

2 Did he use to listen to rap music?

Yes, he did. ☐   No, he didn't. ☐

3 Did he use to eat pasta all the time?

Yes, he did. ☐   No, he didn't. ☐

4 Did he use to have a smartphone?

Yes, he did. ☐   No, he didn't. ☐

5 Did he use to play with his cousins?

Yes, he did. ☐   No, he didn't. ☐

6 Did he use to hang around with his friends in the park?

Yes, he did. ☐   No, he didn't. ☐

2 Do a class survey to find out what your classmates used to do when they were younger. Use the ideas from **1**.

Did you use to play football when you were younger?

No, I didn't.

3 Make a bar chart to show your findings.

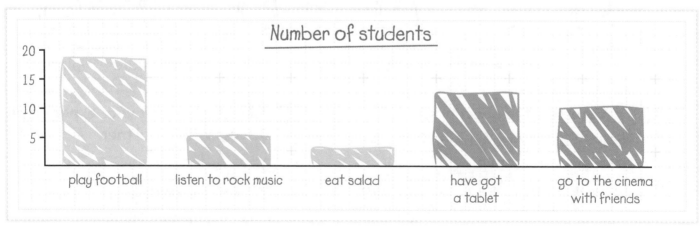

Number of students

play football   listen to rock music   eat salad   have got a tablet   go to the cinema with friends

I can talk about past habits and states.

Writing lab

WRITING A BIOGRAPHY

I will write a biography of someone I know.

1 💬 **Read the biography and answer the questions with a partner.**

My mum is a really inspirational person. She's a nurse who works at the local hospital. She works five days a week and helps people who are ill. She then comes home and looks after me and my younger sister. She's a compassionate person who always thinks of other people. On the days that she doesn't work at the hospital, she is a volunteer at a local animal charity in my town. She does this because she has always wanted to work with animals. After secondary school, she went to university to study Veterinary Science.

She used to enjoy this, but she had to stop her studies to look after her parents who were old and had both become ill. During this time, she realised that she liked looking after people who need help, so she decided to become a nurse. She was brave to do this and it was the right decision.

1 What three adjectives does the author use to describe his mum?

2 What does she do when she isn't at the hospital?

3 Why did she stop studying Veterinary Science?

4 What decision did she make while she was looking after her parents?

2 Think of someone in your family and answer the questions in your notebook.

1 Who is this person?

2 How can you describe their characteristics?

3 Does this person do anything inspirational? What?

4 Did they do anything inspirational in the past? What?

3 Use the information in 2 to write a biography of a family member.

I can write a biography of someone I know.

Make a class book of inspirational people

Project report

1 Read and answer. Then discuss with a partner.

1 Who did you choose as your inspirational person?

_____

2 Why did you choose this person?

_____

3 How did you find out about this person's life?

_____

4 How has this person inspired you?

_____

5 Have you done any inspirational things because of this person?

_____

6 What other adjectives can you use to describe your inspirational person?

_____

7 Did you consider any other inspirational people? If so, who?

_____

2 Complete your project report.

- Inspirational people from the class book: _____

- Facts about these inspirational people: _____

- What did you find difficult about your project? _____

- What did you find easy about it? _____

3 Present your page from the class book to your family and friends.

I can make a class book of inspirational people.

1 Sort and write. Can you add any more words?

author brave campaigner charity worker compassionate determined
generous inspirational intelligent lawyer researcher volunteer

Characteristics	Jobs

2 Complete the sentences with the correct relative pronouns.

1 I once met a boy _____ dad is a famous author.

2 This is the shop _____ I bought that inspirational book.

3 A charity worker is someone _____ works for an organisation such as the Red Cross.

4 My parents were happy _____ I passed the exam.

5 Helping others is something _____ we should all do.

3 💬 Work in pairs. Ask and answer.

1 Where did you use to play when you were younger?

2 When did you use to visit family when you were younger?

3 What did you use to watch on TV when you were younger?

4 How often did you use to go swimming when you were younger?

5 What did you use to do at the weekend when you were younger?

Now go to your Progress Chart on page 4.

1 Checkpoint

1 🎧 011 **Listen and follow Amir's path.**

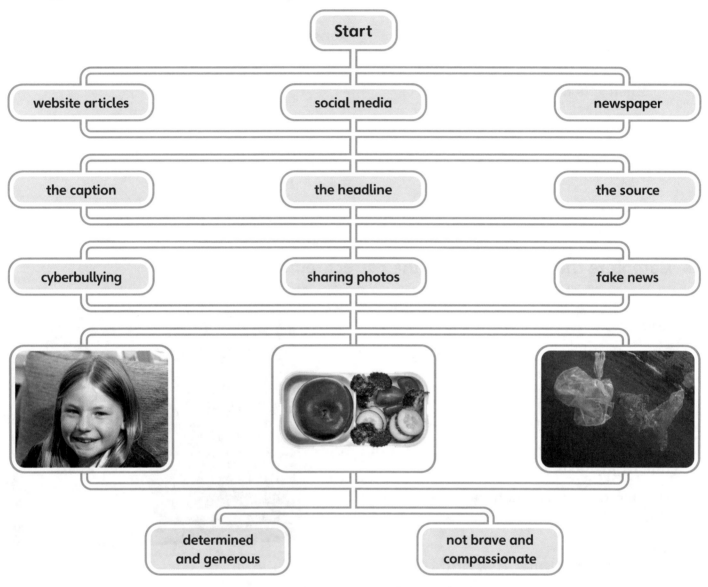

Start

| website articles | social media | newspaper |

| the caption | the headline | the source |

| cyberbullying | sharing photos | fake news |

| determined and generous | not brave and compassionate |

2 **Complete the definitions with words from 1.**

1 _____ : the sentence that describes a photo

2 _____ : online sites where people share information, photos, messages, etc.

3 _____ : a person who likes to share things with others

4 _____ : where information comes from

5 _____ : information that isn't true

6 _____ : willing to do anything necessary to achieve your goal

3 Read the article about Martha Payne and answer the questions.

Young girl helps FEED SCHOOLKIDS

Scottish schoolgirl Martha Payne always wanted to be a reporter. She asked her dad how she could become one, and he said writing a blog was a good way to start. She wrote her first blog when she was nine years old. She uploaded photos of her school meals with captions describing the meals. Martha didn't think the food at her school was healthy or tasty.

One day, a newspaper article wrote about her blog and the school said that Martha could not take any more photos because they were too negative. Martha had to stop blogging, and when her followers heard this, the story went viral. She was determined to continue her blog, and in the end, she was successful. But one reader commented that she was lucky to have food at all. That gave her the idea to use social media for a good cause. She asked her followers if they wanted to donate to a charity to feed hungry children around the world.

She soon had enough money to build a school kitchen in Malawi, which fed all the children at the school for a year, as well as children in other countries.

Martha's story shows how much people can do to help others, no matter how young they are.

1 Where is Martha from?   _____
2 What gave her the idea to start a blog? _____
3 What did she post in her blog?   _____
4 Why did she have to stop blogging?   _____
5 How did she use social media to help people? _____

4 Think about an inspirational person in your country or a young person in the news. Write questions to ask them in an interview.

5 Work in pairs. Role-play your interview and write a short news article.

Student A: You are the reporter.
Student B: You are the inspirational person.

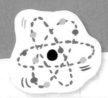

1 **Quickly find the words from the box in the text. Match them to the definitions.**

scientist laureate
degree research
dangerous

1 a detailed study of a subject _____
2 a person who's been given an award for their ability in art or science _____
3 something you get when you finish university _____
4 someone who works with science _____
5 not safe _____

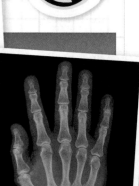

Marie Skłodowska-Curie

The Nobel Prize was the idea of an inventor from Sweden – Alfred Nobel. Until 1903, only men would win. That changed when a Polish scientist called Marie Skłodowska-Curie became the first female winner. She was also the first person to become a double laureate when she won a second Nobel Prize. Her work continues to help people today.

She was born Marie Skłodowska in Warsaw, Poland, in 1867. When she was a child, her family was very poor, but they were intelligent. Both her grandfather and her father were teachers. Marie studied Maths and Physics, and she was a very good student. However, she couldn't go to university in Poland because she was a woman.

In 1891, she went to Paris to attend university, where she studied Physics, Chemistry and Maths. She didn't have much money and life was difficult for her. Her house was very cold, and she was often hungry. Marie was very determined, though, and she finished university in 1894 with degrees in Physics and Chemistry.

She started to work as a scientist and met her husband Pierre Curie. They studied something called radiation. Their research helped to improve X-rays, which can see inside a person's body. Soon hospitals used X-rays to help people and Marie and Pierre won the Nobel Prize for Physics in 1903.

Marie continued to study radiation and X-rays, and in 1911, she won her second Nobel Prize. This time it was for Chemistry. Marie didn't know how dangerous radiation was and she became very ill in 1934. She soon died, but her work has helped many people to live.

2 Read the text in 1 and answer the questions.

1 Where and when was Marie Skłodowska-Curie born?

_____

2 What was her father's job?

_____

3 Why couldn't she go to university in Poland?

_____

4 Why was her life difficult in Paris?

_____

5 Where did she meet her husband?

_____

6 When did she win her first Nobel Prize?

_____

3 Discuss with a partner.

1 Why is Marie Skłodowska-Curie inspirational?
2 How was she determined in her life?
3 How do X-rays help people?

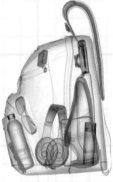

4 Research a Nobel Prize winner. Are there any from your country? Write a biography of this person.

Think about:

- when this person was born
- what their life used to be like when they were young
- what they did to win the Nobel Prize
- why this person is inspirational

5 Present your biography to the class.

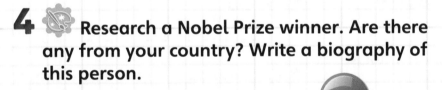

My biography is about …

3 Let's earn money!

How can I make an advertisement for my business?

1 Complete the clues and match. Then use the words to complete the crossword.

Across

1 bake _____

4 sell _____

5 walk _____

Down

2 _____ a T-shirt

3 make balloon _____

5 _____ face painting

2 🎧 012 Listen to the chants. Which two activities are the chants about?

1 _____

2 _____

3 💡 Work in pairs. Which activities in 1 are most popular with adults, children or both? Which of these or other activities have you done?

4 Can you cut the cake into eight equal pieces, using only three cuts of the knife?

CODE CRACKER ⚙️⚙️

Young people in business

VOCABULARY

I will learn words to talk about money.

1 Read and complete.

> advertisement   cash   earn   invented   prices   products   saving   sell   spend

Amy: What can we do for the school fair? Some of the students are going to 1 _____ their artwork. And Rob has 2 _____ a game! We need to think of an idea, too.

Tom: I know! Let's bake some biscuits!

Amy: That's a great idea! We can design an 3 _____ , too.

Tom: Yes, let's do that. People will want to know what ingredients are in our 4 _____ .

Amy: We should include the 5 _____ , too. People should know how much money they need to 6 _____ .

Tom: We need a moneybox to keep all the 7 _____ in, too.

Amy: The fair is a great way to 8 _____ money. What shall we do with all the money?

Tom: We can give it to the school. I know our school is 9 _____ money to buy some new Science equipment.

2 Listen, read and circle.

Frankie hasn't got any 1 **prices** / **products** to 2 **sell** / **spend** . But he's started a business. It's called *Frankie Can Fix It!*

He's made 3 **an advertisement** / **a model** so that people can find out 4 **cash** / **prices** .

He likes to 5 **spend** / **sell** all his 6 **prices** / **cash** on things for his bike. He's 7 **inventing** / **saving** for a new mountain bike. He's also 8 **invented** / **spent** a new bicycle bell. One day, he hopes to 9 **sell** / **earn** money from that, too.

3 How many biscuits did Amy and Tom bake?

MATHS ZONE

Amy and Tom baked some biscuits for the school fair. Lucy bought 3 biscuits and Charlotte bought 2. Mr Wilson bought 12 biscuits. Bella and Scott each bought 6 biscuits. Ms Porter bought 4 biscuits. Tom and Amy shared the biscuits they had left. They each had a biscuit and a half. How many biscuits did they bake for the fair? _____

I can use words to talk about money.

Language lab

GRAMMAR 1: OBLIGATION AND ADVICE

I will learn how to talk about obligation and advice.

1 🎧 014 **Listen. Complete with have to, don't have to, must, mustn't, should or shouldn't.**

Welcome to our school fair!

1.50m

1 You _____ look.

2 You _____ be at least 1 m 50 cm tall.

3 We _____ ask them to paint our faces!

4 You _____ have a tiger's face.

5 We _____ take a plastic bag.

6 We _____ eat them now.

2 Read and complete.

> don't have to   must   mustn't   should   shouldn't

✓ **Do** ... tell the teachers what you are going to sell at the fair.

✗ **Don't** ... come to the playground before 9:00 a.m. (the gates won't be open).

👍 **It's a good idea to** ... write prices on the things. Keep prices low.

👎 **It's NOT a good idea to** ... have expensive prices.

😊 **It's OK. You can** ... buy tickets at the school.

1 You _____ tell the teachers what you are going to sell at the fair!

2 The gates open at 9:00 a.m., so you _____ come to the playground before that.

3 You _____ write prices on things. People like to know how much things cost.

4 To attract more people, you _____ have expensive prices.

5 Tickets will be on sale at the school. You _____ buy tickets online.

3 Write rules and advice. Use each word or phrase only once.

don't have to   have to   must   mustn't   should   shouldn't

1 You _____must_____ stop.

2 You _____ wash your hands in a hospital.

3 You can have lunch at the restaurant. But you _____ eat there. You can have a picnic instead.

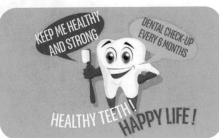

4 You _____ text while you are walking along the street! You might fall.

5 You _____ go to the dentist regularly.

6 You _____ take photos.

4 Work in pairs. Think of a game, board game or sport. Say some rules and tips. Can your partner guess what you are describing?

You have to hit the ball over a net. But you must use your hands. You mustn't drop the ball.

I know, it's volleyball!

5 Think and discuss. Why are rules important? Which rules are most important at home and at school?

I can talk about obligation and advice.

Story lab

♪ THE SCHOOL MUSICAL SHOW! ♪

1 Look and label.

balloon   bottle   bottle top
box   can   card   cup
elastic band   paper
string   tube

2 Read the story again. Match headings 1–5 to paragraphs A–E.

1   Rules of the show   ____

2   It's show time!   ____

3   One day to go ... and we still haven't got an idea!   ____

4   Success!   ____

5   An idea at last   ____

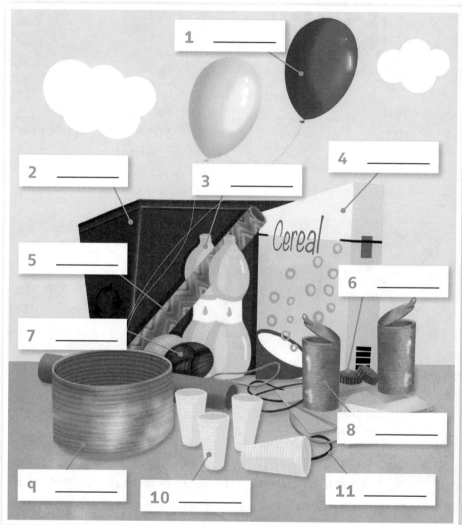

1 ____
2 ____
3 ____
4 ____
5 ____
6 ____
7 ____
8 ____
9 ____
10 ____
11 ____

Cereal

3 Read and circle T (True) or F (False).

1   Lily and her friends had only one week to think of an idea for the school musical show.   T / F

2   Only one person in Lily's group was musical.   T / F

3   Lily had her idea for *The Rubbish Band* on the day of the performance.   T / F

4   The recycling box was outside the classroom window.   T / F

5   Lily's group was the last to perform at the show.   T / F

6   The audience didn't enjoy *The Rubbish Band*.   T / F

4 Read and match.

1 Lily's guitar was made from •
2 The drum was •
3 Hassan was blowing over •
4 The trumpet was •
5 Emir was shaking •

• bottle tops.
• a cereal box and elastic bands.
• a metal can.
• a plastic bottle.
• a cardboard tube.

5 Label the children.

1 _____

2 _____

3 _____

4 _____

5 _____

6 Complete the poster with should, shouldn't, don't have to or must.

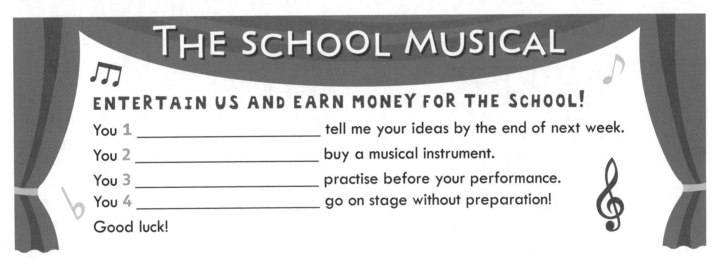

THE SCHOOL MUSICAL

ENTERTAIN US AND EARN MONEY FOR THE SCHOOL!

You 1 _____ tell me your ideas by the end of next week.

You 2 _____ buy a musical instrument.

You 3 _____ practise before your performance.

You 4 _____ go on stage without preparation!

Good luck!

Values Fund our school.

7 Which of these lessons does the story teach us? Discuss in pairs.

Everyone can be creative.

We all have to learn to play a musical instrument.

Rubbish can be useful.

I can understand the sequence of a story.

Experiment lab

I will learn about business.

1 Read and answer.

1   What product did Mr Cheong Choon Ng invent? _____

2   What was in the kits he sold? _____

3   Where did people read reviews of his product? _____

4   In which month did they make a loss? _____

5   In which month did they make a profit? _____

2 Look at the loom band patterns. Which pattern comes next? Circle 1, 2, 3 or 4.

CODE CRACKER ⚙️⚙️

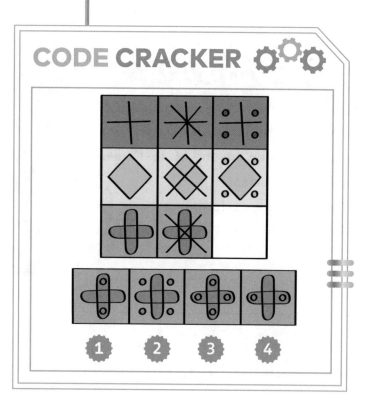

3 Read and complete.

earned   loss   price   profit   sold   spent

Cindy bought 50 pens. She
1 _____ £100 in total. She then
2 _____ each pen for £2.50. She
made a 3 _____ of 50 pence for
each pen.

Jacob designed 25 T-shirts. The T-shirts
cost him £2 each. He sold 10 T-shirts
for a 4 _____ of £4 each and
5 _____ £40. Jacob made
a 6 _____ of £10.

4 ⚙️ Make a coin bag.

5 Read and work out the profit and loss.

1 You bought a plain T-shirt for £3.99. You bought some letters to stick on the T-shirt for £2.50. You want to earn a profit of £4. How much should you sell the T-shirt for?

Cost of T-shirt: _____

Cost of letters: _____

Total cost of T-shirt: _____

Profit: _____

Price: _____

2 Nobody wanted to buy the T-shirt at your selling price. So you sold it for £5. Did you make a profit or a loss?

Total cost of T-shirt: _____

Money you earned: _____

Difference: _____

Is this a profit or a loss? _____

EXPERIMENT TIME

Report

1 Juan sells lemonade for five days. It costs him £4 a day to make the lemonade. He experiments with different prices. Look at the bar chart. On which days does he make a loss? How much is the loss?

Monday £1.25
Tuesday £1.25
Wednesday £1.10
Thursday £1.10
Friday £1.65

 **2** Write your report.

When you *sell* something, you have to think carefully about the _____ .

You can *make* more _____ when something costs more, but you might *sell* fewer products. If you don't *sell* enough to *make* extra money (on top of what you have already spent), you make a _____ .

 **3** Discuss with a partner.

1 How successful was Juan's business?

2 What should he do differently to make more profit?

3 Imagine you've got a business. What would you sell?

I know about business.

Could you do me a favour?

COMMUNICATION: REQUESTS FOR HELP

I will ask and respond to requests for help.

1 Make requests for help. Then match the questions and the answers.

1 borrow / your calculator, / please? / Could / I

_____ ☐

2 help / with my Maths homework, / me / you / Would / please?

_____ ☐

3 please? / you / me / do / Could / a favour,

_____ ☐

4 you / carry this box, / Could / help / please? / me

_____ ☐

5 Would / the way / you / to the station, / please? / show me

_____ ☐

a Of course. Turn left at the end of the street.

b Sure. It's in my pencil case.

c Sure. It looks really heavy!

d Of course. How can I help you?

e Certainly. I'm pretty good at maths!

2 Work in pairs. Practise the questions and answers in 1.

3 Practise asking and answering questions in these situations.

Would you please mark our work, Miss Taylor? — Certainly!

You want your teacher to mark your work.

Your grandfather wants you to help him walk in the park.

Someone wants you to show them the way to a place in town.

You want someone to help you carry your suitcase.

I can ask and respond to requests for help.

Writing lab

WRITING AN ADVERTISEMENT

I will write an advertisement.

1 Read the advertisement and answer the questions.

Do you love comics? Do you dream of being an artist?
Do you read a comic and think, 'Why can't I draw like that?' Well,
now you can — with ComicMaker — the 'make your own comic' kit
for everyone who loves comics!

Each ComicMaker kit comes with an instruction book. Learn how to
draw cartoons and add speech bubbles. We give you a lot of tips to
make the BEST comics in the world!

It's easy, quick and so much fun to do!

Why don't you make them as presents for your friends?

You can buy ComicMaker in all supermarkets and toy
shops, at a price of £12.99.

GO AND GET YOURS NOW!

1 What's the product's name? _____

2 Who is the product for? _____

3 Where can you buy it? _____

4 What's the price? _____

2 Read again and find examples of ...

1 ... a question to persuade us to buy the product. 2 ... an adjective.

3 ... a superlative adjective. 4 ... a fact.

5 ... an opinion. 6 ... an exclamation.

3 Write an advertisement for your product. Include all the information and examples in 1 and 2.

Make a video advertisement for your business

Project report

1 🔧 Read and circle T (True) or F (False).

1 Video advertisements are quick and easy to make.   T / F

2 Written advertisements can be as colourful as video advertisements.   T / F

3 You can see the key words and features of the product more easily
   in a video advertisement.   T / F

4 All the essential information is in one place in a video advertisement.   T / F

5 Video advertisements can tell a story.   T / F

2 Complete your project report.

Our video advertisement is for _____

We included the following examples:

❶ a question: _____

❷ adjectives: _____

❸ a superlative adjective: _____

❹ facts: _____

❺ opinions: _____

❻ an exclamation: _____

We included the following key information: _____

_____

_____

_____

3 💬 Present your video advertisement to your family and friends.

I can make a video advertisement for my business.

1 Read and complete.

advertisement cash earn invent price product save sell spend

Enter our **Young Business Person** competition!

Can you think of a fun or useful 1 _____ that everyone needs? Why don't you
2 _____ something – and then come and 3 _____ it at our business fair!

Make an 4 _____ so that people can see what they are going to get. Don't forget
to tell people the 5 _____ . They have to know how much it's going to cost!

Finally, think about what you are going to do with all the 6 _____ you are going
to 7 _____ at the fair. You can 8 _____ it there – there will be a lot of
interesting things to buy. Or perhaps you want to 9 _____ for a new bike or
a game.

2 Read and complete with have to, don't have to, must, mustn't, should or shouldn't.

School bake sale!

1. No tickets at the gate – book online.
2. CASH ONLY at the fair.
3. Buy a bag – or bring your own bag.
4. It's a good idea to come early.
5. Don't use nuts! (They can be dangerous for many people.)
6. It's not a good idea to put too much sugar in your biscuits.

1 You ___have to / must___ book online.
2 You _____ use cash.
3 You _____ buy a bag.
4 You _____ come early.
5 You _____ use nuts.
6 You _____ put too much sugar in your biscuits.

3 Work in pairs. Ask and answer.

1 What do you like to spend your spare cash on?
2 Do you ever save money? What would you like to buy one day?
3 What is more important to you: earning money or enjoying your job?

Now go to your Progress Chart on page 4.

1 Look at the nutrient groups. Add three more examples to each group.

Carbohydrate	Protein	Fat	Fibre
pasta	fish	olive oil	whole grains

2 Listen to the radio documentary and complete the sentences. Use one or two words.

1 We might have to eat certain foods in the future because the planet _____ .

2 People don't _____ in the USA and Europe.

3 Insects contain protein and _____ .

4 If we eat more insects, we won't have to cut down so many _____ .

5 Seaweed is good before and after exercise because it contains a lot of _____ .

6 The jackfruit tree doesn't need much _____ .

7 The problem with lab-grown meat is that it is too _____ .

3 Look and complete.

CODE CRACKER

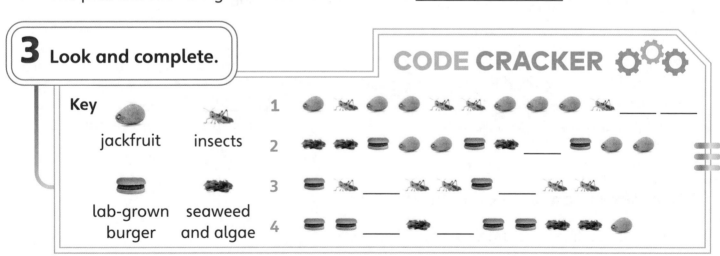

Key

jackfruit   insects

lab-grown burger   seaweed and algae

4 Make an incomplete pattern. Give it to a partner to complete.

Food and farming

VOCABULARY

I will learn about food and farming.

1 Look and label.

> fruit and vegetables   intensive farming   meat and fish   organic farming
> pesticides   pollinators   sugary foods   sustainable farming

_____

_____

_____

_____

_____

_____

_____

_____

_____

_____

_____

_____

_____

_____

_____

_____

EXTRA VOCABULARY

2 Find out the meaning of the words. Then complete the sentences.

> famine   food waste   hunger

1 This is when too much food is produced or bought and some has to be thrown away. _____

2 This is when there isn't any food in a country to eat for a long time. A cause is often the weather.

_____

3 This is the feeling a person has when they haven't got enough to eat. _____

3 Ph 016 Listen and write the words in the correct category.

aw sound	oo sound
_____	_____
_____	_____
_____	_____
_____	_____
_____	_____

I can use words to talk about food and farming.

Language lab

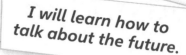

I will learn how to talk about the future.

1 Read and circle.

1 ' I'm going to meet / I'll meet / I'm meeting Sara at the café on Saturday. We arranged it a few days ago', said Maria. ____

2 David has decided that he isn't going to give up / won't give up / isn't giving up meat. ____

3 'I'm quite hungry!' 'Don't worry, I'm going to make / I'll make / I'm making you something to eat.' ____

4 Many believe that people aren't going to have / won't have / aren't having enough to eat in the future. ____

5 'She's made up her mind! She's going to eat / She'll eat / She's eating less sugar.' ____

6 'That cake you've made looks really nice.' 'If you wait a moment, I'm going to give / I'll give / I'm giving you a slice to try.' ____

7 'Does your brother want to come to the market with us?' 'He can't. He's going to go / He'll go / He's going to the cinema with his friend.' ____

8 'What are we going to have / will we have / are we having for dinner tonight, Mum?' 'Rice and fish.' ____

2 Are the sentences in 1 a prediction (PR), an intention (I), a plan (PL) or a decision made at the time of speaking (D)?

3 Write questions. Then ask and answer the questions with a partner.

1 people / eat insects every day in my country / in five years?

_____

2 you / meet friends / this weekend?   _____

3 you / eat less meat / in the future?   _____

4 where / you go on holiday / this summer?   _____

4 Read what Jack is thinking. Complete the sentences with will, be going to or the Present Continuous and the correct form of the verbs.

eat less sugar

study hard to pass my exams

become captain of the football team next year

meet with friends at the new burger restaurant this weekend

visit grandparents after school today

drink some juice – I'm suddenly very thirsty!

1   Jack _____ less sugar. He thinks it is very bad for our health.

2   He thinks he _____ captain of the football team next year. He's been training very hard.

3   He _____ with friends at the new burger restaurant this weekend. They made plans yesterday.

4   He's suddenly very thirsty. He _____ some juice.

5   He _____ hard to pass his exams. He wants to go to university.

6   He _____ his grandparents after school today. He goes every Wednesday.

5   Write a sentence describing what you intend to do after school today, a sentence about what your plans are this weekend and a sentence describing what you think you will do in the future. Discuss with a partner.

1   _____

2   _____

3   _____

6 Write your partner's sentences from 5.

1   _____

2   _____

3   _____

I can   talk about the future.

Story lab

READING

I will read a science-fiction story.

The tiny robots

1 Find these words in *The Tiny Robots*. Tick ✓ the picture that best describes each word.

greenhouse

a   b   ☐

gardener

a   b   ☐

crops

a   b   ☐

2 🔧 **Number the events in the correct order.**

a ☐ The crops in the greenhouses now had a lot of fruit and vegetables.

b ☐ Fatima asked her dad to build bee robots.

c ☐ Fatima's dad designed and built the agriculture robots.

d ☐ Fatima had an idea about how to solve the problem.

e ☐ Iris told Fatima that no pesticides were used in the colony.

f ☐ Fatima and her family moved to the colony on Mars.

g ☐ The human gardeners were worried because the crops were failing.

3 Complete the sentences to summarise the story.

1 Fatima's favourite place in the colony was _____.

2 The greenhouses reminded Fatima of _____.

3 Fatima liked to watch _____.

4 They were going to run _____.

5 Iris told Fatima that there were no _____.

6 The bee robots pollinated _____.

4 Discuss the questions with a partner.

1 Why do you think humans are living in a colony on Mars?

2 Why are they growing crops in a greenhouse?

3 Why aren't the crops growing well?

4 How are the jobs of the agriculture robots and the bee robots different?

5 017 Read and listen to the text. Answer the questions.

1 Why are pollinators so important?

2 What will happen if there are no pollinators?

3 How can we look after pollinators?

hummingbird

wasp

bat

The loss of pollinators

Some small animals are really important for the survival of the human race. Why? Because they are pollinators and without them flowers, plants and trees will die. But what are pollinators? Insects like bees, wasps and flies, and animals like bats and hummingbirds. They help flowers, plants and trees to pollinate. This means they are able to make new flowers, plants and trees. Pollinators help to make fruit and vegetables, which we eat. No pollinators means no apples or tomatoes, for example. We are losing many pollinators. Many millions of bees have died recently. We aren't sure exactly why this is, but it is believed to be because of a number of reasons: disease, pesticides and humans have destroyed many areas where bees live. We have to look after pollinators because without them we won't survive.

6 Read and answer.

MATHS ZONE

Values Food sustainability.

7 What can we all do to help pollinators? Discuss with a partner.

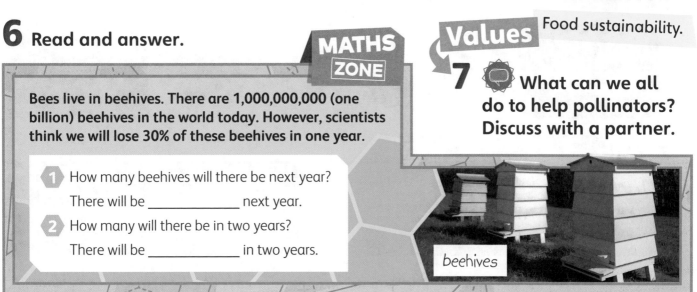

Bees live in beehives. There are 1,000,000,000 (one billion) beehives in the world today. However, scientists think we will lose 30% of these beehives in one year.

1 How many beehives will there be next year?
There will be _____ next year.

2 How many will there be in two years?
There will be _____ in two years.

beehives

I can read a science-fiction story.

Experiment lab

SCIENCE: FOOD CHAINS

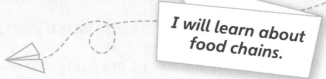

I will learn about food chains.

1 **Read and complete.**

primary consumer   producer   quaternary consumer
secondary consumer   tertiary consumer

1   These are normally large
    carnivores which only eat meat. An example of this is a lion.   _____

2   These organisms are normally herbivores, like small insects,
    that only eat plants and grass. An example of this is a locust.   _____

3   These are at the top of some food chains and they eat tertiary
    consumers. An example of this is a human.   _____

4   This is an organism that is at the bottom of the food chain.
    It gets its food from the Sun. An example of this is grass.   _____

5   These are in the middle of most food chains and they are omnivores,
    which means they eat plants and meat. An example of this is a frog. _____

2 **Label the food chain. Use the words in 1.**

1 _____ → 2 _____ → 3 _____ → 4 _____ → 5 _____

3 **Number the photos to create two food chains. Use 1 for the bottom of the food chain and 4 for the top of the food chain.**

A

☐ leopard   ☐ locust

B

☐ rat   ☐ slug

☐ grass   ☐ baboon

☐ owl   ☐ leaves

4 Listen to the podcast about food chains in different habitats. Answer the questions.

1 What is a habitat?
2 In which continent can you find the savannah?
3 What producer in the savannah does the podcast mention?
4 What animal eats this producer?
5 What animals eat the primary consumers?
6 What tertiary consumer does the podcast mention?

5 Look at the organisms that live in a tundra habitat. Draw arrows to show the direction of the food chain.

6 Make a paper food chain.

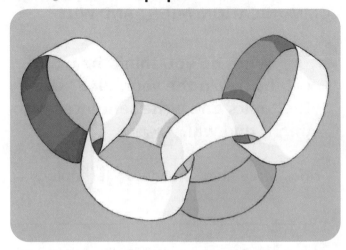

EXPERIMENT TIME

Report

1 Draw and label the sea food chain.

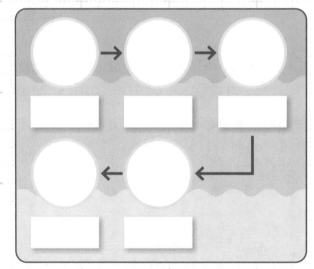

2 Think about your experiment. Discuss with a partner.

- What worked?
- What went wrong?
- What will you do differently next time?

I know about food chains.

It might rain!

COMMUNICATION: *MITHT AND WILL*

1 What do you think the world will be like in the year 2045? Use the topics and write sentences with **might** and **will**.

cities   free time   holidays   technology

1 _____

2 _____

3 _____

4 _____

2 Discuss your ideas with a partner.

We might live in cities under the sea in 2045.

We will go to the Moon for our holiday.

3 Think about food and farming in the future. Work with a partner and research one of the topics. Make notes.

LAB-GROWN MEAT   INSECTS   VEGAN FOOD   MEAT AND FISH   ORGANIC FARMING   PESTICIDES

4 Present your research to the class. Remember to use **might** and **will**.

5 Play *What am I predicting?*

I can talk about future possibilities.

Writing lab

WRITING ABOUT AN EVENT IN A NEWSLETTER

I will write a newsletter entry.

1 Read the newsletter. Circle the food stall that doesn't serve animal products.

SMITHSON FOOD FESTIVAL

Are you coming to the annual Smithson Food Festival next week? Will you eat the best food you've ever eaten? We're sure you will! There will be more than 20 food stalls at the festival, including:

- **JOE'S SEAFOOD SHACK.** Try the finest fish and seafood at Joe's Seafood Shack. Splendid salmon, beautiful prawns and so much more!

- **THE VEGAN HOUSE.** Are you tired of eating meat? Then come to the Vegan House to try our animal-free food, such as vegan burgers, vegan curry and our special vegan pizza. You won't eat anything healthier … or tastier.

- **IRENE'S INSECTS.** Will you be brave enough to try something different? Are you going to accept the challenge and eat fried locusts? You'll be surprised how nice insects are.

- **A TASTE OF SPAIN.** You'll remember your favourite holiday in Spain when you try our delicious Spanish food. Tortilla, paella, churros … We've got it all!

THE SMITHSON FOOD FESTIVAL WILL TAKE PLACE IN THE TOWN SQUARE ON 22–25 MARCH. SEE YOU THERE!

2 Read and answer.

1 Underline the future forms.
2 Why are some words in bold?
3 Why does the writer use bullet points?

3 Think of an event near you. Answer the questions.

- What type of event is it? _____
- What will be there? _____
- What's the date and time? _____

4 Use the newsletter in 1 and your answers in 3 to write a newsletter.

I can write a newsletter entry.

Create a 3D plan of a sustainable farm for the future

Project report

1 Compare your 3D plan of a sustainable farm for the future with a partner's. What is the same or different?

	My sustainable farm	My partner's sustainable farm
What foods will the farms produce?		
How will the farms be sustainable for the future?		
What materials were used?		

2 Complete your project report.

- Our report is about: _____
- We used the following sources to find information:

  _____

  _____

- Examples of visuals in our report include:

  _____

  _____

- We used the following materials in our 3D plan:

  _____

  _____

3 Present your report to your family and friends.

I can create a 3D plan of a sustainable farm for the future.

1 Choose three words. Write sentences with these words missing. Can your partner guess the words?

> carbohydrate   fat   honey   intensive farming   jackfruit   organic farming
> pesticides   pollinators   protein   sugary foods   sustainable farming

1 An organic farmer doesn't use _____ because they kill insects.

2 _____

3 _____

4 _____

2  Write one sentence describing what you intend to do after school today and one sentence describing what you think you will do in the future. Discuss with a partner.

1 _____   2 _____

3 Look at Diana's diary for next weekend. Complete the sentences.

○ SATURDAY A.M.
○ Play tennis with Marta ✓

○ SATURDAY P.M.
○ Meet Marcus at the restaurant ?

○ SUNDAY A.M.
○ Walk the dog in the park ?

○ SUNDAY P.M.
○ Do school project with Juan ✓

1 Diana _____ play tennis with Marta on Saturday morning.

2 She _____ meet Marcus at the restaurant on Saturday afternoon. She isn't sure at the moment.

3 She _____ walk the dog in the park on Sunday morning. This depends on the weather.

4 She _____ her school project with Juan on Sunday afternoon.

4 What are you doing this weekend? What might you do? Talk with a partner.

5 Tell a partner about three interesting things you have learnt in this unit.

Insects contain a lot of protein.

Pollinators are very important for humans.

2 Checkpoint
UNITS 3 AND 4

1 🎧 019 Listen and follow Maya's path.

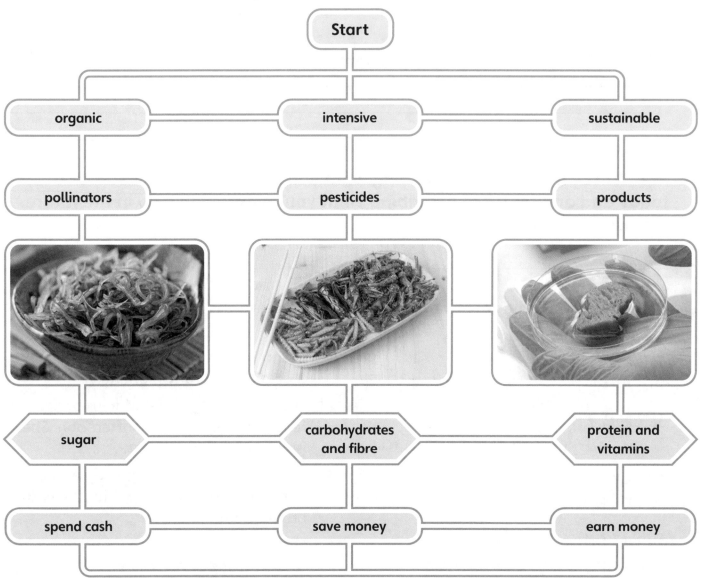

Start

| organic | intensive | sustainable |

| pollinators | pesticides | products |

| sugar | carbohydrates and fibre | protein and vitamins |

| spend cash | save money | earn money |

2 Complete with words from the flowchart.

1 Bees and butterflies are natural _____ .

2 Organic farmers don't use _____ on their crops or in the soil.

3 _____ farming isn't sustainable.

4 People can buy _____ like honey and biscuits at the fair.

5 Algae and seaweed are forms of _____ we get from the sea.

6 When you sell something, you _____ from it.

3 Read and answer.

We're having A FOOD FAIR!

We're going to start an organic garden at our school. Please help save money to buy seeds, soil and equipment! There will be a lot of exciting new products to try at our fair next month.

Scientists say that intensive farming isn't sustainable. For this reason, we should all try to eat less meat. So, come and try:

- jackfruit burgers! Special offer – two for the price of one!
- homemade lemonade – with honey instead of sugar
- delicious seaweed biscuits

All our products come from organic farms – so it's all free from pesticides.

Note: You don't have to buy tickets in advance – we will sell tickets on the day.
We haven't got a card machine, so you must bring cash. (a lot of it ☺)

ONLY CASH please :)

1   What kind of text is this – an advertisement or a newsletter entry?   _____

2   Is one jackfruit burger more expensive than two?   _____

3   What advice does the text give us about our future diets?   _____

4   Why will the lemonade be healthier?   _____

5   What is the benefit of using organic fruit and honey?   _____

6   Is it necessary to buy tickets in advance?   _____

4 Invent a product or service for a school fair. Write a short description of it and answer these questions.

1   How can you earn money from it? _____

2   What is the price? _____

3   What do people have to know about the product or service?

_____

5 💬 Work in pairs. Ask and answer about your ideas.

What are you going to do for the fair?

I'm going to collect shells and little stones, and make bracelets.

1 Read. Where are the majority of flower farms in Kenya? _____

MY SCHOOL PROJECT –
Flower farms in Kenya
by Jomana Salah

Farming is an important industry in Kenya. Farmers grow coffee, tea, fruit such as pineapples and vegetables like sweet potatoes. They export a lot of these products to other parts of the world. Farmers also grow flowers and the Kenyan flower industry is the third biggest in the world after the Netherlands in Europe and Ecuador in South America. Let's find out more about it!

WHY IS FLOWER FARMING SO IMPORTANT?

Flower agriculture – or floriculture, which is its real name – is important to the economy of Kenya. There are more than 200 flower farms in the country and these employ nearly 100,000 people.

WHERE DO THEY SEND THE FLOWERS TO?

Every day, these farms send their fresh flowers to countries in Europe, as well as the USA and Russia.

WHAT TYPES OF FLOWER DO THEY EXPORT?

Well, if you receive a rose on your birthday, maybe it came from Kenya. The other main types of flower they export are carnations and lilies.

WHERE ARE THE FLOWER FARMS IN KENYA?

All over the country, but mainly around Lake Naivasha, which is in the Great Rift Valley near the capital, Nairobi. This is one of the largest lakes in the country.

rose

IS FLORICULTURE IN KENYA SUSTAINABLE?

In the past, the flower farms used so much water from Lake Naivasha that it was nearly dry. Today, the industry is more sustainable than in the past. Farmers don't use much water from the lake. They use recycled water instead. A lot of farms also use solar energy from the Sun.

ARE THE FARMS ORGANIC?

carnation

Some are. They don't use harmful pesticides or other chemicals, which can pollute the land and kill plants and trees. You can find a lot of pollinators such as bees in these farms. These pollinators help to create more flowers.

So, when you next think about farming, remember that it's not just food.

2 Read and circle T (True) or F (False). Correct the false sentences.

1   Farmers in Kenya export a lot of their products around the world.   T / F

_____

2   The flower industry in Kenya is the second largest in the world.   T / F

_____

3   Nearly 100,000 people work in flower farms in Kenya.   T / F

_____

4   Lake Naivasha is the largest lake in Kenya.   T / F

_____

5   The flower industry in Kenya is less sustainable now than in the past.   T / F

_____

3 Read and complete. Use some of the blue words in 1.

Farming in my country

Farmers in my country grow a lot of things like tea, fruit
and vegetables. There are also a lot of Fair Trade farms.
They 1 _____ a lot of things to different countries
around the world. My country is the biggest exporter of rice
and potatoes.

Farming in my country is mainly around the coast. This is because it is too hot inland.
Farms are normally 2 _____ . They use 3 _____ water from the sea.
Many farms are also organic. They don't use chemicals that can 4 _____ the sea.

4 Research and write a description of farming in your country. Use the texts in 1 and 3 to help you.

Think about:
- what they grow
- if they export
- where they export to
- if it is sustainable
- if it is organic

5 Present your description to the class.

The ancient world

How can I make an audio tour guide about the past?

1 Complete the words.

1 p____ p____ r____ ____
2 h____ e ____ ____ g ____ y ____ h ____ cs
3 c ____ f ____ ____ n
4 ____ u ____ m ____

2 Look at 1 and find words that mean …

a   … the preserved body of a person or animal. ☐

b   … a container for a preserved body. ☐

c   … ancient Egyptian writing. ☐

d   … ancient paper made from a plant. ☐

3 Read the hieroglyphics to work out the words.

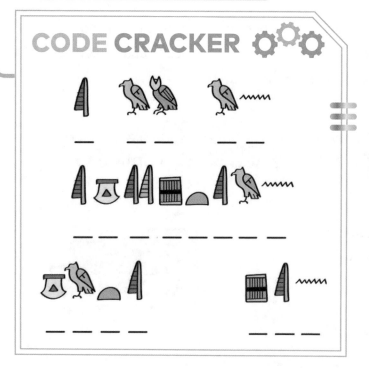

CODE CRACKER

4 Work out the ancient sum.

MATHS ZONE

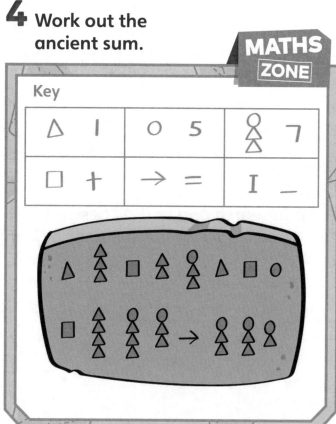

Key

△	1	○	5	(symbol)	7
□	+	→	=	I	_

Ancient Egypt

VOCABULARY

I will learn words to describe life in ancient Egypt.

1 Read and complete.

archaeologist coffin hieroglyphics hole
mummy papyrus pyramid treasure

In 1922, the British **1** _____ Howard Carter made a discovery. He was digging
a **2** _____ in a part of Egypt called the Valley of the Kings. Suddenly, he saw
something. It was a **3** _____ ! The ancient Egyptians often built a **4** _____ as the
burial place of a pharaoh. But the burial place of King Tutankhamun was deep underground.
Carter couldn't believe what he discovered inside. It was the **5** _____ of the famous
pharaoh! Carter also found something else underground. There were more than 5000 pieces
of **6** _____ – gold, statues and jewellery. The walls of the underground burial place
were full of **7** _____ – the ancient Egyptian writing. This paper was made from a plant
called **8** _____ . Carter's discovery became one of the most famous in world history.

2 020 Listen and choose the correct answer.

1   Why wasn't King Tut's burial place
    a pyramid?

   a   Because he was only 18 when he died.

   b   Because there wasn't time to build
      a pyramid.

3   When did Carter start digging the hole?

   a   in 1922

   b   in 1914

2   What did the hieroglyphics on the
    cup spell?

   a   King Tut's name

   b   the location of King Tut's burial place

4   Why did he have to stop digging
    for several years?

   a   The war started.

   b   There was no more money.

EXTRA VOCABULARY

3 Read and match.

1   They found the mummy in a **tomb**.
2   People paid a **scribe** to read and write for them.
3   The precious **artefacts** are in the Egyptian museum.

a   objects from history
b   someone who reads and writes letters
c   a burial place

4 Ph 021 Listen and sort the words with the same sounds.

| hurt wear bear there |
| work pear fur burn |

Group 1 (*turn*)	Group 2 (*where*)
_____	_____
_____	_____

I can use words to describe life in ancient Egypt.

Language lab

GRAMMAR 1: PAST PASSIVE

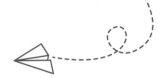

I will learn about the Past Passive.

1 🔄 022 **Write sentences using the Past Passive. Then listen and check.**

1   People grew papyrus beside the River Nile.

Papyrus _____was grown_____ beside the River Nile.

2   People used the plant to make a lot of different things: shoes, clothes, medicine, blankets, perfume and books!

The plant _____ to make a lot of different things.

3   That's why people called it 'the gift of the Nile'.

That's why it _____ 'the gift of the Nile'.

4   The Egyptians glued strips of papyrus together and they created a long piece of writing material.

Strips of papyrus _____ together and a long piece of writing material _____ .

5   Then they tied each end to a stick of wood.

Then each end _____ to a stick of wood.

6   When they covered the papyrus with writing, they rolled 'the scroll' up and put it inside a tube.

When the papyrus _____ with writing, 'the scroll' _____ up and _____ into a tube. Some scrolls were more than 50 metres!

2 Complete the sentences in the Past Passive.

1   100,000 people built the Great Pyramid at Giza.

_____

2   They used 2,300,000 stone blocks to build the pyramid.

_____

3   We still don't know exactly how they carried these heavy stones.

_____

4   Pharaoh Khufu ruled Egypt at that time.

_____

5   He gave the workers food.

_____

3 Complete the sentences. Then work in pairs and circle T (True) or F (False).

1 Egyptian boats _____ (make) of papyrus.   T / F
2 Three mummies _____ (find) inside the Great Pyramid at Giza.   T / F
3 Eye make-up _____ (wear) by men and women.   T / F
4 Egyptian houses _____ (build) of stone.   T / F
5 Ancient Egypt _____ (rule) by about 170 pharaohs.   T / F
6 Food _____ (keep) in holes underground to stop thieves.   T / F
7 Bread and onions _____ (eat) only by rich people.   T / F

4 🔧 Listen and check.

5 🔧 Listen again and correct the false sentences in 3.

_____

_____

_____

_____

6 How many stones were used to build the pyramid?

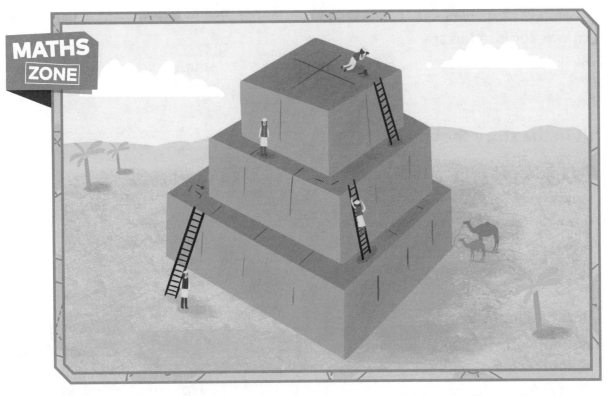

MATHS
ZONE

I can use the Past Passive.

Story lab

READING

> I will read a story about a boy and his dream.

☆ A good night story ☆

1 🔊 **024 Listen and choose the correct answer.**

1   Yusuf was reading

    a   an adventure story.   b   a true story.   c   a modern Egyptian story.

2   Why couldn't Yusuf see what was in front of him?

    a   Because it was dark.   b   Because there was a small door in front of him.   c   Because he was in a very small room.

3   What was the meaning of the gold eagle?

    a   It was an item of jewellery.   b   It brought good luck.   c   It told archaeologists that King Tut was in that burial place.

4   When Yusuf woke up

    a   it was morning.   b   it was dark.   c   he was in the pharaoh's burial place.

5   Yusuf's mum was surprised to see

    a   the book in his hands.   b   the curtains closed.   c   a small gold statue of an eagle.

2 Find words in the story that mean …

1   … something you use to help you see in the dark. _____

2   … part of a building that helps you to walk down to a lower level. _____

3   … pictures, drawings or paintings. _____

4   … the top part of a room. _____

5   … something that you imagine while you are sleeping. _____

3 Look at the diagram. Write the letters.

1 Which room was full of hieroglyphics and ancient Egyptian scenes? ____

2 Which room was full of treasure? ____

3 Where was Yusuf standing when he switched on his torch? ____

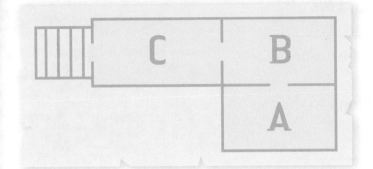

4 What do you think happened next in the story? Write a paragraph. Then compare with a partner.

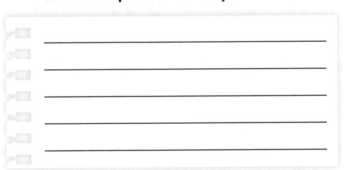

5 Work in pairs. How often do you remember a dream? Tell each other about a dream you remember.

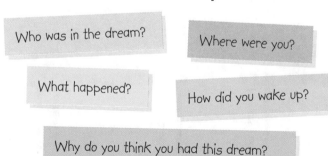

Who was in the dream?

Where were you?

What happened?

How did you wake up?

Why do you think you had this dream?

6 Make a paper pyramid!

7 Can you find the way out of the maze?

CODE CRACKER

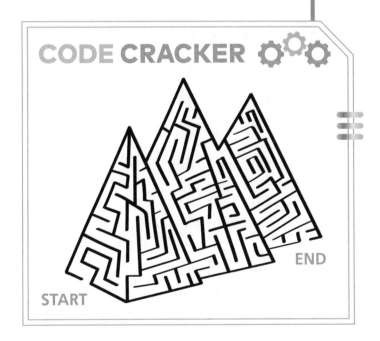

START

END

 I can read a story about a boy and his dream.

Experiment lab

I will learn about force and friction.

1 Read and answer. Use the words in the box.

> force   friction   logs   molecules   a ramp   ropes   rough sand   a sledge

1   After the stone for the pyramids was cut, what form of transport took it to the building site? _____

2   What objects were used to make this form of transport? _____

3   What structure did they build to move the stone to the top of the pyramid? _____

4   What did they use to pull it up? _____

5   What material was used to build this structure? _____

6   What was created when the sledge moved over the rough sand? _____

7   What objects in water attach to each other to reduce friction? _____

8   When there was less friction, what was reduced to help pull the stone along the sand? _____

2 Discuss in pairs.

1   Look at the picture of the sledge. Why did logs make it easier to pull the sledge?

2   Would more force be necessary to pull a sledge made with square blocks instead of logs? Why?

3 Work in pairs. Look at the pictures and discuss.

1   Which situation needs more force to move the books, a or b?

2   Can you think of everyday situations when a ramp is used?

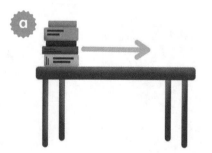
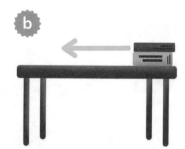

EXPERIMENT TIME

Report

1 Think and write about your experiment.

- What worked? _____
- What went wrong? _____
- What will you do differently next time? _____

2 Read about force and friction. Then write your report.

> Force is a push or pull to make an object move in a certain direction. To move an object along a flat surface from a low level to a higher level, we use a ramp. When the object moves along a surface, it causes friction. The shape, size and weight of an object have an effect on the friction and force needed to move the object.

FORCE AND FRICTION

1 _____ objects cause less friction.

2 _____ objects cause more friction.

3 More force is needed to move an object along a _____ surface.

4 Less force is needed to move an object along a _____ surface.

5 Dry sand causes _____ .

6 Wet sand causes _____ friction because _____ .

3 Try some more experiments with ramps. Write the results of your experiment in the table.

What object did I use?	What surface did I make?	Results
a heavy, rough stone	smooth (metal)	
a round cardboard tube	rough (carpet)	

I know about force and friction.

73

A tour back in time

COMMUNICATION: PAST PASSIVE QUESTIONS

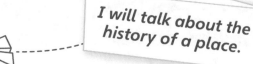

I will talk about the history of a place.

1 **Look at the photo and the questions. Write the questions in the Past Passive.**

1 When did they build it?

_____

2 Who ruled Rome at that time?

_____

3 What did they use the building for?

_____

4 What food did they serve there?

_____

5 How did they keep the building cool in hot weather?

_____

6 What damaged the building?

_____

The Colosseum, Rome

2 **Work in pairs and guess the answers.**

3 025 **Listen. Did you guess correctly?**

4 **Write the questions in the Past Passive in your notebook. Then match.**

1 Where did they find the first dinosaur fossils? ☐   a the ancient Chinese

2 When did they invent the first pair of glasses? ☐   b around 1885

3 Who used the first alarm clock? ☐   c in England

4 Where did they discover the world's oldest pyramids? ☐   d the ancient Greeks

5 Who invented paper? ☐   e in Brazil

6 When did they make the first car? ☐   f 1268–1300

5 026 **Now listen and check.**

6 **Write your own quiz questions in your notebook. Ask the class. Who can get the most correct answers?**

I can talk about the history of a place.

Writing lab

WRITING A FACT FILE

I will write a fact file.

1 Read the fact file and answer the questions.

THE ANCIENT INCA SITE OF MACHU PICCHU, PERU

- Machu Picchu means 'Old Mountain' in Quechua, the language that was spoken by the Incas.

- The city was built in the mid-1400s.

- It is known as the 'Lost City of the Incas' because it wasn't discovered until 1911 by an American historian called Hiram Bingham.

- To stop the city from sliding down the side of the mountain, more than 600 large, flat steps (called terraces) were made.

- Between 300 and 1000 people lived in the city for about 100 years in the fifteenth century. They moved away from Machu Picchu in the 1500s.

1   What does the name Machu Picchu mean?   _____

2   When was it built?   _____

3   Why is it known as the 'Lost City of the Incas'?   _____

4   How was the city stopped from sliding down the mountain?   _____

5   When was it discovered and by whom?   _____

2 Find at least one example from the fact file to match the topics.

1   Information about the name of the place

2   Important dates and what happened

3   Facts about the construction

4   Interesting information about the people who lived there

3 Plan. Choose a famous place. Write notes about each of the topics in 2.

4 Write your fact file about a famous place.

I can   write a fact file.

PROJECT AND REVIEW UNIT 5

Make an audio tour guide about the past

Project report

1 Think about your project. Discuss in pairs.

1 What facts do you think are the most interesting?
2 Where did you do your research?
3 How many sources did you use?
4 How did your introduction make listeners interested in finding out more?

2 Complete your project report.

① What local area was chosen for your project?

_____

② How did you learn about the history of that area?

_____

③ What were the questions you asked to find out interesting information?

_____

④ List the topics your project covers in the right order.

_____

⑤ List at least three facts.

_____

⑥ Find an example of how something was made, discovered, built, etc.

_____

3 Present your report to your family and friends.

I can make an audio tour guide about the past.

1 Complete the sentences in the Past Passive and with words you find in the word search.

l	n	d	j	y	u	n	k	s	z	c	d	o
h	i	e	r	o	g	l	y	p	h	i	c	s
p	a	p	y	r	u	s	e	t	b	j	c	i
a	r	c	h	a	e	o	l	o	g	i	s	t
p	y	r	a	m	i	d	c	o	f	f	i	n
l	t	r	e	a	s	u	r	e	h	o	l	e
b	u	r	i	a	l	m	u	m	m	y	b	a

1   When an ancient Egyptian pharaoh died, his body _____ (preserve) as a _____ .

2   The preserved body _____ (put) into a wooden container. _____

3   This container _____ (decorate) with Egyptian writing. _____

4   Egyptian writing was usually on paper called _____ , which _____ (make) from a plant.

5   The container _____ (take) to a _____ place.

6   A tall, stone triangular structure _____ (build) at this place. _____

7   In 1922, an amazing discovery _____ (make) by Howard Carter, as he dug a _____ in the ground in the Valley of the Kings.

8   The discovery was found alongside 5000 objects of _____ – gold, jewellery, statues, etc.

2 Write questions. Then ask and answer in pairs.

1   King Tut's mummy / take / to a pyramid as a burial place?
    Was King Tut's mummy taken to a pyramid as a burial place?

2   When / King Tut's mummy / discover?
    _____

3   Who / it / discover by?
    _____

4   Where / the hole / dig?
    _____

5   How many treasures / find / underground?
    _____

6   What / paint / on the coffin?
    _____

Now go to your Progress Chart on page 4.

6 On the move!

✈ How can I help exchange students in my town?

1 Look at the photo and answer the questions.

1 What can you see?
2 Why do you think the boy is there?
3 How do you think he is feeling?
4 How does the photo make you feel?

2 Check that you know the airport words below. Write two more.

> bus   car park   check-in
> departure gate   security   terminal
> _____   _____

3 Write definitions for your two words. Read the definitions to a partner. Can they guess the words?

1 _____
2 _____

4 ⚙ Listen to the conversation at a departure gate in an airport. Answer the questions.

1 What was the first problem for James?
2 What happened when he got to check-in?
3 Where was his passport?
4 Why did the security guard stop James?

5 Help James get to check-in, through security and then to the departure gate to meet Melania. Draw a path using arrows ⬆⬇⬅➡.

- Use each square only one time
- Don't use squares with ✕

CODE CRACKER ⚙⚙

Start here		✕		Security	
					✕
	✕		✕		
		Check-in			Departure gate
✕			✕		

Airports and travel

VOCABULARY

I will learn words for places in an airport.

1 Read and complete.

> check-in   departure gate   luggage
> passport   security   takes off   terminal

A JOURNEY ↘ THROUGH AN AIRPORT

When a traveller arrives at an airport to catch a plane, they first go to the correct **1** _____
and then to **2** _____ . Here, the traveller's **3** _____ and other documents are looked
at. Also, any **4** _____ is weighed before it goes on a special machine to the aeroplane.
The traveller goes through **5** _____ and makes their way to the **6** _____ . They get
on the plane, which shortly **7** _____ to its destination.

EXTRA VOCABULARY

2 Look and label the picture below.

> aisle   aisle seat   emergency exit
> flight attendant   overhead locker
> seatbelt   window seat

3 Ph 028 Listen and repeat. Which word doesn't belong? Which sound is it?

1   fire   wire   flour   tyre
2   require   power   hourglass   our
3   overpower   iron   sunflower   tower
4   entire   empire   wire   sour

1 _____   2 _____   3 _____   4 _____   5 _____   6 _____   7 _____

EXIT

Language lab

GRAMMAR 1: PRESENT PERFECT CONTINUOUS

I will learn about the Present Perfect Continuous.

1 **Complete the sentences with the correct form of the words in brackets.**

1   I _____ (wait) here for more than an hour!

2   He _____ (not feel) well since he woke up this morning.

3   'How long _____ (you/live) here?'
    'Oh, for about five years.'

4   It _____ (rain) since yesterday.

5   'How long _____ (he/study) English?'
    'Since he was five.'

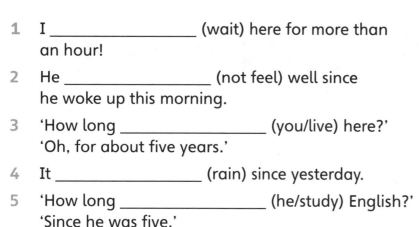

2 **Circle the correct words to complete the sentences.**

1   They've been playing tennis for / since 12 o'clock.

2   I've been doing my homework for / since two hours.

3   Has Olivia been living here for / since 2017?

4   We've been planning our holiday for / since months.

5   He's been eating that pizza for / since nearly an hour!

3 **Write sentences using for or since.**

1   Pedro / study / five o'clock

    _____

2   Elena / train / for this race / last summer

    _____

3   I / live here / I was born

    _____

4   we / come here / years

    _____

5   she / think of / emigrating / the middle of December

    _____

4 🗨 🎧029 **What is the difference between emigration and immigration? Discuss with a partner. Then listen and complete the notes.**

Emigration is when _____ _____ .

Immigration is when _____ _____ .

5 🎧029 **Listen again. Complete what the people are saying.**

1 'How long have people been _____ to other countries?'

2 'I think they have been doing this _____ a very long time.'

3 'We think humans have been _____ for 200,000 years.'

4 'It's because conditions in other countries are sometimes _____ than in our own.'

5 'People sometimes move to join their _____ in a different country.'

6 **Read and solve the maths problem below.**

MATHS ZONE

People have been moving from country to country for many thousands of years. Every year in the UK, people leave to live elsewhere and people come from a different place to live in the country. The population of the UK at the start of 2019 was 67,141,684. During the year, 351,000 people emigrated, but 625,000 decided to move to the UK.

What was the population of the UK at the end of 2019? _____

7 🗨 **Work with a partner. Give a reason for situations 1–4.**

1 She looks tired.

2 He's cold.

3 You're very, very hungry.

4 They're hot.

She looks tired.

She's been travelling for eight hours.

I can use the Present Perfect Continuous.

Story lab

I will read a comic strip story.

LOST!

1 Look at the words from the story. Choose five of them and write a correct and an incorrect definition for each. Give your definitions to a partner. Can they choose the correct definition?

> for ages   miss   to spot   sweets   a trail
> security announcements   anxious   teddy bear   the rest

2 Discuss with a partner.

1   When was the last time you felt anxious? What made you feel this way?

2   How often do you eat sweets? What type is your favourite?

3   What haven't you done for ages?

4   Have you ever missed someone that you haven't seen for a long time? Who?

5   Did you use to have teddy bears when you were younger? If so, describe one.

3 Read and circle T (True) or F (False). Correct the false sentences.

1   Alex and his family have been planning their move to Vietnam for a long time.　　T / F

_____

2   Alex's mum has been working in Hanoi for six months.　　T / F

_____

3   Alex has been missing his mum a lot.　　T / F

_____

4   Amelie has been eating a lot of sweets.　　T / F

_____

5   Alex follows the trail of sweets out of arrivals.　　T / F

_____

6   Amelie has been riding on someone else's bicycle.　　T / F

_____

4 Which is the route that Dad and Alex followed? Look and tick ☑.

a
security   restaurants and cafés   departures   ☐

b
departures   passport control   restaurants and cafés   ☐

c
departures   restaurants and cafés   arrivals   ☐

5 Listen to the conversation between Alex and his mum when he arrives in Vietnam. Where is the flat?

6 What was Alex's life like in the UK? How will it be different in Vietnam? Listen again and make notes.

	The UK	Vietnam
House		
Place		
Food		
School		

7 Which do you prefer: Alex's life in the US or his life in Vietnam? Discuss with a partner.

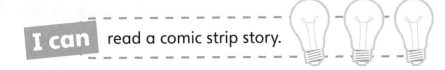

I can read a comic strip story.

Experiment lab

TECHNOLOGY: IRIS RECOGNITION

I will learn about biometric technology.

1 Read and match.

1. The coloured part of our eyes •
2. No two irises •
3. Biometrics is a type of technology •
4. You can find iris recognition •
5. An iris scanner matches your iris •

• in airports, for example.
• is called the iris.
• to information in a database.
• are the same.
• that looks at the unique features of the body.

2 What conclusion does the author of *Iris Recognition* come to?

3 🔊 031 Read and listen to the text about another type of biometrics. Can a person's fingerprints be the same as someone else's in the world?

FINGERPRINTS

You see iris recognition in airports and you use voice recognition with your smartphone. So, if you think that biometrics is a recent technological advance, you're wrong. We've been using biometrics for decades.

HOW? Take a very good look at your fingers. The shapes in the skin of your fingers are called fingerprints and police use these to identify criminals. When police go to the scene of a crime, they check if the criminal has left any fingerprints. If so, these can be used to identify the criminal.

HOW? Everyone's fingerprints are different. There are three types of fingerprint shape – arch, loop and whorl. For each person, these are slightly different, so what you see on your fingers is unique to you.

Despite this, using this type of biometric to capture criminals is not perfect. Innocent people have sometimes been sent to prison because of a mistake by the police. They've found other fingerprints at the scene of the crime and arrested the wrong person. Biometrics help to keep us secure and they make life easier for many, but we mustn't trust them 100% all the time.

arch

loop

whorl

4 Use the steps below to check your fingerprints. Compare them with the rest of the class.

1 Rub the pencil on paper. Press your finger down onto the paper and move it from side to side.

2 Press your finger onto the sticky side of the tape. Then stick the tape onto the other piece of paper.

3 Has your fingerprint got an arch, a loop or a whorl?

What you need:

- a pencil
- two pieces of paper
- a piece of sticky tape

5 Go online to research answers to the questions below. Then discuss with a partner.

1 We use iris recognition in airports. Where else do we use iris recognition?

2 What are the advantages of using biometrics?

3 What are some disadvantages of using biometrics?

4 How do you think biometrics will be used in the future?

EXPERIMENT TIME

Report

1 Complete the graph below.

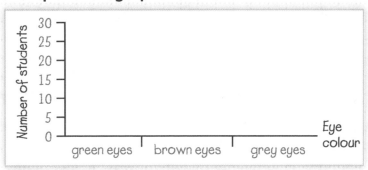

2 Think about your experiment. Discuss with a partner.

- What worked?
- What went wrong?
- What will you do differently next time?

 about biometric technology.

Have we arrived yet?

COMMUNICATION: *JUST, ALREADY, YET, STILL*

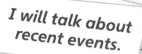

1 Juan now lives in a different country. Complete the text about his first few days in his new home. Use **just, already, yet** or **still**.

We've **1** _____ emigrated to a new country because my dad got a new job. I **2** _____ haven't started a new school because it's the summer holiday. My sister has **3** _____ made a lot of friends in the neighbourhood, but I haven't made any **4** _____ . Dad has **5** _____ started his new job. It was his first day yesterday and he was so nervous. Mum is looking for work, but she hasn't found anything **6** _____ .
I **7** _____ haven't sent my friends from home my new address. I promise I'll do this tomorrow!

2 Complete the table below with information from 1.

This has happened	This hasn't happened
1 _____ We've just emigrated. _____	1 _____
2 _____	2 _____
3 _____	3 _____
	4 _____

3 Copy and complete the table in 2 with things you have done and things you haven't done this week. Remember to use **just, already, yet** and **still**.

4 💬 Discuss your table with a partner.

I have already done my Maths homework.

I haven't done mine yet!

I can talk about recent events.

Writing lab

GIVING FEEDBACK

I will write a feedback form.

1 Read the online reviews for a hotel. Which reviews are negative and which are positive?

| Hotel Reviews | Restaurant Reviews | Write a review | More ... | 🔍 Search |

Best place ever ★★★★★

I've just spent three nights at your amazing hotel. Can I just say that the experience was wonderful? My husband and I were impressed by everything at your hotel, but the best thing was the helpful receptionist. It was our first time in your city but, luckily, the receptionist gave us a lot of helpful recommendations. Thank you! *Mrs Janssen, Copenhagen*

Disgusting ★☆☆☆☆

Unfortunately, I stayed at your hotel during a visit to the city for work and I still haven't recovered from the experience. Firstly, it was so noisy that I couldn't sleep. The other hotel guests made so much noise! I complained to reception, but they didn't seem interested. Secondly, the food was terrible. I ate in the restaurant, which was a dreadful experience. My dinner wasn't cooked and then my breakfast was cold. Never again!

Simon Timpson, London

Brilliant room service ★★★★☆

There are many good things about your hotel. It's clean and it's near the city centre, but I think the best thing is the room service. I was very hungry, so I ordered something to eat late at night. Thankfully, the food arrived within five minutes. I will return to your wonderful hotel. *Gulia, Milan*

2 Read the reviews again. Circle the adverbs that show a sequence of events and underline the adverbs that add emphasis.

3 💬 Think about all the bad things that can happen when you stay at a hotel. Use the reviews in 1 to help you. Discuss with a partner.

4 Write your review of a bad experience. Remember to use adverbs that show a sequence of events and adverbs that add emphasis.

5 💡 Read your review to the class. Who had the worst experience?

I can write a feedback form.

Create a welcome pack to help exchange students to settle in

Project report

1 Answer the questions.

1 What information surprised you about your nearest airport?

_____

2 What did you need to think about when you were deciding what help Luke and Gabby needed in the airport?

_____

3 Was it more difficult to think about the help that Luke needed or that Gabby needed?

_____

4 Why do you think Luke/Gabby gave you the feedback that they did?

_____

5 How did you decide what information about yourself to include in the welcome pack?

_____

6 What other information did you include in your welcome pack? Why did you include that information?

_____

7 Was it easier to be the Welcome Buddy or Luke/Gabby in the role-play? Why?

_____

2 Complete your project report.

- My report was about:

  _____

- Examples of visuals in my welcome pack include:

  _____

- I used the following sources to find information:

  _____

- I used the following materials in my welcome pack:

  _____

3 Present your report to your family and friends.

I can create a welcome pack to help exchange students to settle in.

1 Look through the unit. Find and write:

1 Four words related to airports and travel:

_____ _____

_____ _____

2 An adjective to describe someone who is worried about something:

_____

3 Three fingerprint shapes:

_____ _____

_____

4 Four things you can find inside an aeroplane:

_____ _____

_____ _____

5 A verb that means to be sad about not seeing someone for a long time:

_____

6 Two types of biometrics:

_____ _____

2 Think and discuss.

1 What's the difference between the verbs *to take off* and *to land*?

2 How are emigration and immigration different?

3 Why do some people move to another country?

4 What is biometrics?

5 Why do we normally give feedback?

3 Complete the sentences with the correct form of the words in the box.

look for   study   travel   watch   wear

1 They _____ for ages, but they still haven't arrived.

2 She _____ hard, so she might not pass the exam.

3 Have you seen my glasses? I _____ them, but I can't find them.

4 We _____ a brilliant TV series. It's called *Crime City*. It's so exciting.

5 _____ (you) my coat? I don't know where it is.

4 Work with a partner. Imagine you are late for your lesson. Think of as many excuses as possible.

Sorry we're late. We've been studying in the library.

Now go to your Progress Chart on page 4.

3 Checkpoint
UNITS 5 AND 6

1 032 Listen and follow Amir's path.

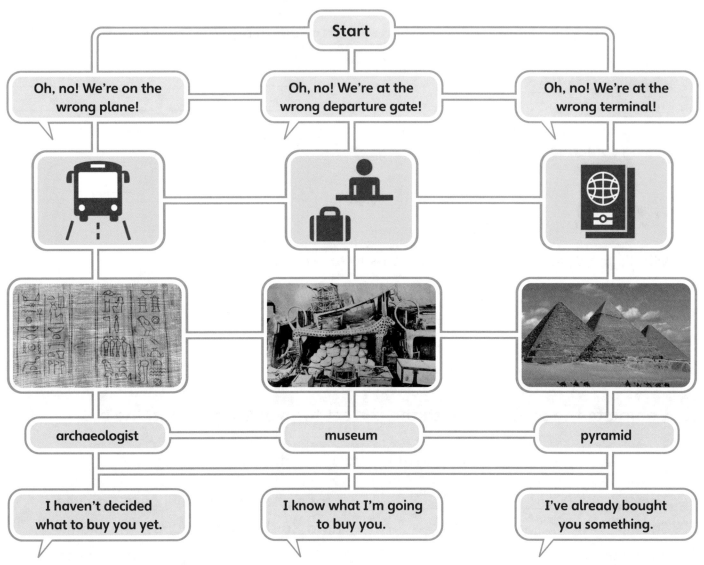

Start

Oh, no! We're on the wrong plane!

Oh, no! We're at the wrong departure gate!

Oh, no! We're at the wrong terminal!

archaeologist

museum

pyramid

I haven't decided what to buy you yet.

I know what I'm going to buy you.

I've already bought you something.

2 Complete with words from 1.

1   Show your ticket and hand in your luggage at the _____ desk, before you get on the plane.

2   A _____ was the burial place of many pharaohs.

3   An _____ digs in the ground to find ancient objects.

4   Some very big airports have got several different 'mini airports' or _____s.

5   Passengers wait at the _____ before they get on the plane.

3 Read Amir's feedback about his trip to Luxor. Answer the questions.

Our trip to Luxor was one of the best parts of my holiday in Egypt. Of course, the highlight was the Valley of the Kings. A tip for anyone who is planning to visit: take a torch! The underground rooms were very badly lit and you can't take photos, so a torch is useful. I also recommend the Luxor Museum. It was opened in 1975. In the Luxor Museum, you can see several of the treasures that were found in King Tut's burial site. But the best thing about the museum is the mummies of two pharaohs, Ahmose I and Ramesses I. Interestingly, these were only put in the museum when a new part was built in 2004. I also enjoyed my visit to the second floor, where visitors can see exactly how papyrus was grown and then made into paper. Don't miss the 16 statues that were discovered by archaeologists working at Luxor Temple in 1989.

1 Why did Amir find a torch useful?

2 When was a new part of the building added?

3 What was put in the new part?

4 What can visitors learn about on the second floor?

5 Where were the 16 statues discovered? By whom?

4 Choose one famous place and write a fact file.

THE LIGHTHOUSE OF ALEXANDRIA

- Who built it and when? Pharaoh Ptolemy II, in the third century BCE.
- Where? It's on the island of Pharos, just off the coast of Alexandria.
- How did the light work? A fire provided the light.
- What happened to the building? Earthquakes damaged it between 956 and 1323 CE.
- Who discovered it again, and when? In 1968, archaeologists discovered parts of the building.

THE CAIRO TOWER

- When? 1956 to 1961.
- Where? In the middle of Cairo.
- Who designed it? Egyptian architect Naoum Shebib.
- What does it look like? A lotus flower, which ancient Egyptians used to make papyrus.
- When and how did they restore it? Between 2004 and 2009; builders added four more floors and a lift.

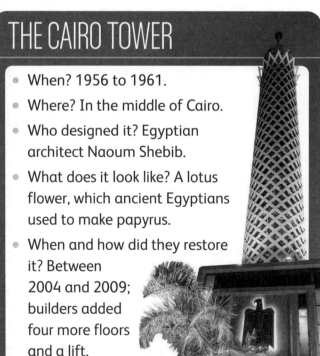

5 Work in pairs. Ask and answer about the place your partner wrote about.

1 Find the words in the text. Write definitions in your own words.

1 treasures _____

2 relics _____

3 cutlery _____

4 remains _____

5 extinct _____

6 fossil _____

2 Read *Oxford and Its Museums*. In which museum can you see ancient pottery?

OXFORD AND ITS MUSEUMS

Oxford is a small city in the southeast of England. It's home to the oldest university in England, the University of Oxford, which is also one of the oldest in the world. In the city centre, there are many attractive, historic buildings, which all belong to the different colleges that the university consists of. Many tourists from around the world visit Oxford every day to see these buildings, many of which can be seen in films and TV series. There are also two famous museums in Oxford, both of which belong to the university.

The Ashmolean Museum

This is one of the oldest museums in the world. It first opened in 1678 to show the public of Oxford some of the university's treasures. Inside the Ashmolean, you can see many important relics from different periods in history. From ancient Egypt, there are mummies and sculptures of important people, and different pieces of pottery. Some of these are nearly 3000 years old. You can also find Japanese clothes and jewellery, which are about 600 years old, paintings done by Native Americans and sixteenth-century plates and cutlery from the Middle East.

The Museum of Natural History

This is near the Ashmolean, so you can visit both in the same day. This museum opened in 1860 and is famous for its collection of very old, strange animals. Here you can find the only existing remains of the dodo. This was a large bird from New Zealand that became extinct in the eighteenth century. There are fossils of dinosaurs that have been found near Oxford, as well as a replica skeleton of the most famous dinosaur of them all: the tyrannosaurus rex!

3 Read again and answer the questions.

1   Why do a lot of tourists visit Oxford?

_____

2   Why did the Ashmolean Museum open?

_____

3   What relics from ancient Egypt can you see in the Ashmolean Museum?

_____

4   When did the dodo become extinct?

_____

5   Which museum is older: the Ashmolean or the Museum of Natural History?

_____

4 Read again. Complete the table below with the correct information. Write *NG* if the information is not given.

	British Museum	Ashmolean Museum	Museum of Natural History
First open?			
How many pieces in collection?			
Famous pieces in collection			

5 Research and write a description of a museum that you know in your country.

Think about:
- when the museum first opened
- how many pieces are in the collection
- what famous pieces are in the collection

The museum I chose is the Huntington History Museum. It's a small museum in ...

6 Present your description to the class.

1 Look, read and complete.

bees   get lost   heights   skyscraper   slip on

A: Look at that brave window cleaner, working on a _____ !

B: I know! I could never do that. I'm afraid of _____ .

A: How are we going to get there?

B: Let's look up the directions. I don't want to _____ .

A: Oh, no. He's going to _____ a banana skin!

A: Let's pick some of these wild flowers.

B: No! I'm scared of _____ .

2 Listen to Li Na and her friend playing a game. Circle Li Na's answers, *a* or *b*.

WHICH IS SCARIER?

a standing on the balcony of a skyscraper

b riding up to the top of a skyscraper in a glass lift

WHICH IS SCARIER?

a sleeping alone in a tent

b camping in a cave with bats

WHICH IS SCARIER?

a forgetting your words when you're performing on stage

b falling over in front of people

3 Can you solve the puzzle?

MATHS ZONE

A frog has fallen off the wall into a hole. The hole is 30 metres deep. Each day the frog jumps 3 metres up the side of the hole. He sits there for the rest of the day. Every night when he falls asleep, he slips backwards 2 metres. How many days does it take the frog to get out of the hole?

Oh, no!

VOCABULARY

I will learn words to describe challenging situations.

1 Read and circle.

1 It was so funny when Max (forgot) / (called) his teacher 'Mum'.

2 I (texted) / (forgot) my words on stage and the audience just looked at me.

3 Jim is nervous about the camping trip because he has never (looked down) / (slept) in a tent before.

4 I'm sorry I'm late for class! I didn't hear my alarm clock and I (turned off) / (overslept)!

5 How embarrassing! I realise now that I (slipped) / (texted) my friend Dan instead of my dad last night.

6 I couldn't send you an email last night. My mum (texted) / (switched off) the internet at 10 p.m.

2 🔊 034 Listen. Which situation from 1 are the speakers talking about?

EXTRA VOCABULARY

3 A phobia is a very strong fear of something. What are people with these phobias scared of?

1	aerophobia ●	●	open spaces
2	claustrophobia ●	●	spiders
3	arachnophobia ●	●	planes
4	bibliophobia ●	●	books
5	agoraphobia ●	●	enclosed spaces

4 Ph 🔊 035 Listen. Circle the silent letters.

comb   eight   height   knee   know   tomb   write   wrong

Values Challenge yourself.

Are you afraid of oversleeping? You should set two alarms!

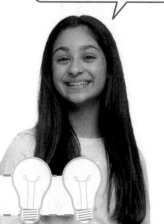

5 Discuss in pairs. Give advice to a partner about one of the situations in 1.

I can use words to describe challenging situations.

Language lab

I will learn about the Present Perfect and Past Simple.

1 Complete the sentences with the correct form of the verbs in brackets.

1 I _____ (go) to London twice before.

   I _____ (fly) there last year and the year before.

2 I _____ (never see) a kangaroo.

3 I _____ (lose) my train ticket last week. Now I have to buy a new one.

4 My sister loves that book. She _____ (read) it four times already.

5 This is the most delicious pizza I _____ (ever eat).

6 Clara is late for class. It's unusual. She _____ (never oversleep) before.

7 I _____ (never live) anywhere else except this town.

8 Have you seen a black and white cat? He _____ (run) away four days ago. We still _____ (not find) him.

2 Write questions in the Present Perfect.

Have you ever ...?

1 find money in the street   _____

2 forget to study for a test   _____

3 drop all your books   _____

4 cry while watching a film   _____

5 fall off a chair in a restaurant _____

6 use salt in your tea instead of sugar _____

7 oversleep on an important day   _____

3 Play *Did it really happen?*

Have you ever found money in the street?

Yes, I have.

When did that happen? Where did you find it? What did you do with it?

4 Six children have visited different countries. Use the clues to complete the table.

1. Jack has not visited Europe.
2. Dan has not been to Africa.
3. Frank has not visited Portugal or France.
4. Piotr and Tina have visited Africa, but they haven't been to Europe.
5. Piotr hasn't travelled to Morocco.
6. Jack and Tina have not visited Senegal.
7. Scott has not been to France or Spain.
8. Tina hasn't been to Morocco.

Name of person	Country
	Portugal
	Senegal
	Kenya
	France
	Morocco
Frank	Spain

Africa: Senegal, Kenya, Morocco

Europe: Portugal, France, Spain

5 Write questions about experiences. Use the verbs in the box or your own ideas.

drop   fall asleep   feel   forget   get   give   go
lose   miss   oversleep   see   send   wave

Have you ever waved at the wrong person?

6 Make a question spinner. Play with a partner.

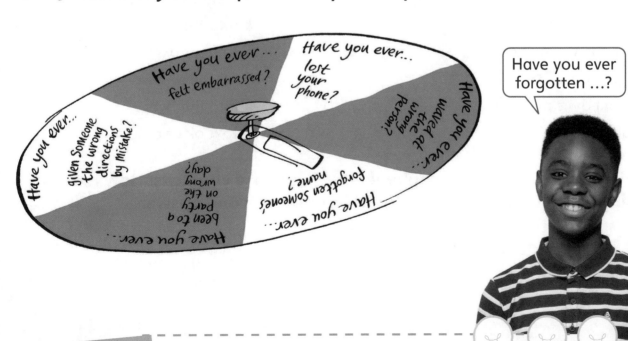

Have you ever... felt embarrassed?

Have you ever... lost your phone?

Have you ever... given someone the wrong directions by mistake?

Have you ever... been to a party on the wrong day?

Have you ever... forgotten someone's name?

Have you ever... waved at the wrong person?

Have you ever forgotten ...?

Story lab

I will read a conversation.

The challenge

1 **Read and circle T (True) or F (False). Correct the false sentences.**

1   Josie called Luis because they were going to be late.   T / F

_____

2   When Josie called Luis, he was looking for a smooth stone.   T / F

_____

3   Luis got lost while he was walking through the forest.   T / F

_____

4   Josie and Luis took a photo of the nest.   T / F

_____

5   Josie screamed because she was angry.   T / F

_____

2 Read and match.

1   Josie wanted to go •   • through the forest.
2   Luis fell •   • from the snake.
3   He sat on the grass •   • into the tunnel.
4   Luis took the wrong path •   • to get dry.
5   He climbed a tree •   • on the grass.
6   Luis dropped his phone •   • into the river.
7   Josie ran away •   • to look at a nest.

3 **Write your own Nature challenge list. Compare your lists. How many of the things on the lists have you done? In pairs, ask and answer.**

4 Look at the story map. What went wrong? Draw the parts of the story that are missing. Then write the captions.

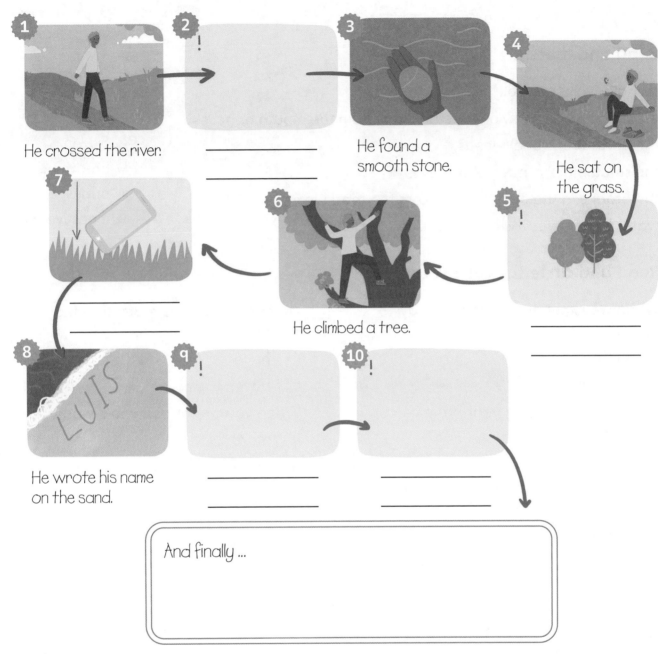

1. He crossed the river.
2. _____ _____
3. He found a smooth stone.
4. He sat on the grass.
5. _____ _____
6. He climbed a tree.
7. _____ _____
8. He wrote his name on the sand.
9. _____ _____
10. _____ _____

And finally ...

5 Compare with a partner.

I drew Josie running away from the snake. What about you?

I drew Luis and Josie crossing the finish line.

I can read a conversation.

Experiment lab

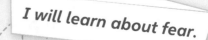
I will learn about fear.

1 Read and match.

1 standing still, not able to move ●
2 the process of air moving into the lungs from the mouth or nose ●
3 the air that our body needs ●
4 the small black centres of our eyes ●
5 the organs in the body that process the food we eat ●
6 water that leaves the body through the skin ●

● sweat
● oxygen
● frozen
● breathing
● pupils
● digestive system

2 Read and circle the correct answer.

1 When we experience fear, our body prepares for
   a flight.
   b fight or flight.

2 Humans … always reacted to fear this way.
   a have
   b haven't

3 When you are afraid, your brain can't think about
   a the scary situation.
   b anything except the scary situation.

4 When you are afraid, you breathe
   a more slowly.
   b more quickly.

5 You can see more clearly because your pupils grow
   a bigger.
   b smaller.

6 The … slows down.
   a heart
   b digestive system

3 What effects is fear having on the person and the cat in the pictures? Tell your partner.

The boy is sweating.

4 Draw Ryan's heart rate on the bar chart.

Ryan's pulse is 80 beats per minute, before he does any exercise. Then he runs slowly for one minute and his pulse goes up to 120 beats per minute. He skips for another minute and his pulse goes up to 170 beats per minute. He then rests for two minutes, and his pulse drops to 140 beats per minute.

	0	10	20	30	40	50	60	70	80	90	100	110	120	130	140	150	160	170
Resting																		
Running																		
Skipping																		
Resting																		

EXPERIMENT TIME

Report

1 Write your report. Were your results the same as your predictions? What did you guess correctly?

> I predicted that running on the spot would make my heart beat faster than walking around the room. I was correct.

What worked well?

_____

What didn't work?

_____

2 What other exercises would you add to the experiment next time? Can you predict the results? Discuss.

I know about fear.

I'm going to talk about …!

COMMUNICATION: GIVING A PRESENTATION

I will learn about giving a presentation.

1 **Match the examples from the presentation to the headings.**

a Introduce the topic

b Use personal experiences and order your points

c End the presentation

1   **I'll never forget** the first time I took a trip in a plane. **It was when** I was about five. ☐

2   **To summarise, then,** fear is something we all feel, but it isn't always a negative thing. ☐

3   The first thing I remember is feeling weak at the knees. I couldn't move! **Then** I noticed how my heart was beating faster and I was sweating. I was so scared, I really didn't enjoy the flight at all. ☐

4   **I'd like to talk about** fear – what is fear, and how does it make us feel? ☐

5   **On the other hand,** some of my most enjoyable times have been watching horror films with friends. We're usually terrified, but because we are together, it's fun! ☐

2 🎧 036 **Listen and check.**

3 **Read the advice. Which advice are the speakers in the pictures following or not following?**

- Learn the speech.
- Speak clearly and loudly.
- Write key points on cards.
- Make eye contact!

4 **Research, write and give a short presentation about fear. Use the phrases in bold in 1 to help you.**

I can give a presentation.

Writing lab

WRITING A DIALOGUE

I will write a dialogue.

1 🔊 037 Choose the correct lines of the dialogue a–d to go before the sentences 1–4. Then listen and check.

Ivan is going to visit his friend, Kim. He rings the doorbell.

1 ☐ Ivan walks into the living room. He stops, amazed. Kim is playing a game of chess – with a dog!

2 ☐ Ivan sits down and watches the game for a while. He is shocked.

3 ☐ **Kim:** (*moving a chess piece carefully*) You can't believe I'm going to win the game?

4 ☐ **Kim:** (*gives a short laugh*) He's not very intelligent at all. We've played three games already, and I've won all of them!

a **Ivan:** (*more loudly*) No, it's not that. Maybe you will win … but I still can't believe you're playing chess with a dog! He must be the most intelligent dog in the world.

b **Ivan:** (*whispering, amazed*) But … I can't believe my eyes!

c **Kim:** (*calling from inside*) Come in! The door is open.

d **Kim:** (*not looking up*) Hello, Ivan! How are you? Sit down, please. I'll win and the game will be over soon. I've got some great moves planned!

2 ⚙ Research and plan a dialogue. Use a mind map to write notes.

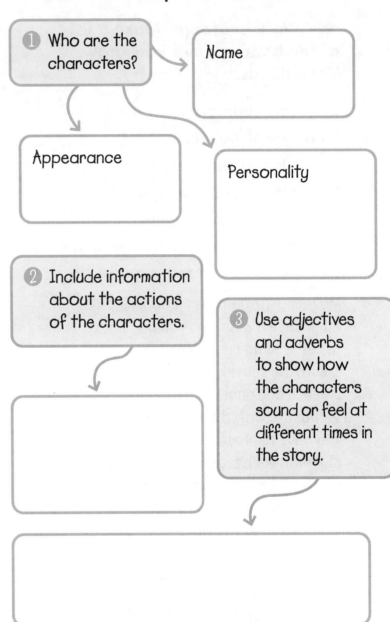

① Who are the characters? → Name

Appearance

Personality

② Include information about the actions of the characters.

③ Use adjectives and adverbs to show how the characters sound or feel at different times in the story.

3 Use your notes to write a dialogue.

4 💬 Work in pairs or groups and role-play your dialogues.

I can write a dialogue.

Design and make a board game about fears

Project report

1 💬 Work in groups. Make a list of the board games you know. Then discuss.

1 Which are your favourite games?

2 What do you like about them?

3 When do you play these games?

4 How many players can play?

5 What are some of the rules?

6 How long does each game take to win?

My favourite game is *Pictionary*. I like it because it's fun and you don't have to count or add numbers. I often play it with my cousins. You need a board, a pencil and paper. You can play *Pictionary* with three or more people. You have to play in two teams. One player in each team has to draw a word and the other players in the team have to guess what it is. Sometimes you can guess the word quickly, but sometimes it's very difficult!

2 💡 Compare your board game with another well-known board game. What features are similar or different?

how many players

what you need

rules

how to play

3 Complete your project report.

- Our game is for:
  _____

- To play our game, you need:
  _____

- The rules are as follows:
  _____

- The winner is the player who:
  _____

4 💬 Present your game to your family and friends.

I can design and make a board game about fears.

1 Complete the sentences about the situations. Use the Present Perfect and the Past Simple.

1 What has happened?

She ___has overslept___ because she _____went_____ to bed late last night.

2 He is nervous because he has to give a presentation, but he _____ what to say.

3 Oh, no! I've _____ a cup of coffee all over my desk!

4 She's nervous because she _____ a mountain before.

2 Work in pairs. Play *Charades*.

3 Make your own *Find someone who ...* game. Write a list of experiences, then ask your classmates to find *who*. Ask for details.

Find someone who ...

Name	Experience	Specific details
Elena	has eaten snails	She ate them in a French restaurant.

Now go to your Progress Chart on page 4.

8 My amazing city

How can I create a project to change my city?

1 Listen to a tour guide describe a city to some tourists. Choose the correct option to complete the sentences.

1 Some of the buildings in the city are nearly _____ years old.

   a 200   b 1200

2 One of the oldest buildings in the city was once a _____ .

   a restaurant   b bank

3 The building opposite the restaurant is part of the _____ .

   a university   b shopping centre

4 The Simpson Tower skyscraper _____ the tallest building in the country.

   a is   b was

2 Look at the map of the city and imagine you are a tour guide. Plan a trip for tourists.

Where should the tourists go?	
If rainy: _theatre_ or _park_	If sunny: _____ or _____
If young tourists: _____ or _____	If old tourists: _____ or _____

CODE CRACKER

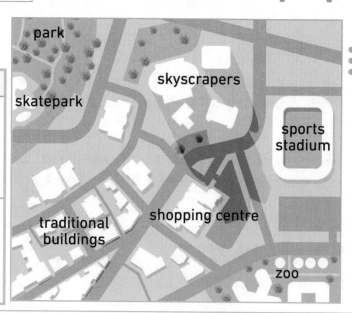

3 Create a 3D map of your city. Describe it to a partner.

> There are some skyscrapers and a shopping centre.

City centre

VOCABULARY

I will learn words for buildings and structures in towns and cities.

1 Read and complete the fact file about the city of Liverpool in the UK.

skyscraper   stadiums   statue
tunnels   universities

LIVERPOOL

- The world's oldest _____ is in Liverpool. Today, it isn't even the tallest building in the city, but it inspired the famous Empire State Building in New York and the Burj Khalifa in the United Arab Emirates.

- There are two football _____ in the city – Goodison Park, where Everton FC play, and Anfield, where Liverpool FC play. Everton FC played at Anfield before Liverpool FC existed!

- There is a big river in Liverpool called the Mersey. Three _____ go under the river. Cars and other road vehicles use two of them and trains use the other.

- There are four _____ in the city and students from all over the world come to study at them.

- A famous band called The Beatles came from Liverpool. Today, you can see a _____ of the four members of the band in the city centre.

EXTRA VOCABULARY

2 Use a dictionary to find out what the words mean. Then complete the sentences.

bustling   cosmopolitan
run-down   touristy   unspoilt

1   This part of the city is really _____ . There are a lot of souvenir shops and many chain restaurants. There's nothing for local people.

2   I love this city because it's so _____ . You can eat food from anywhere in the world and you hear people speak so many languages.

3   There are no modern buildings or shopping centres in this part of the city. All the buildings are traditional. It's really _____ .

4   The old part of the city isn't very nice. There's litter everywhere, the streets are dirty and a lot of the shops are closed. It's very _____ .

5   The city centre is really _____ at night. Everything is open, there are a lot of restaurants and there are people everywhere.

I can use words for buildings and structures in towns and cities.

Language lab

GRAMMAR 1: SECOND CONDITIONAL

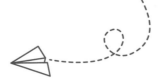

I will learn the second conditional.

1 Read and circle the correct words.

1 If I lived / (would live) in a skyscraper, I would (use) / used the lift every day!

2 If I am / (were) rich, I ('d) / 'll buy a house near the beach.

3 If she (knew) / knows the answers, she'd (pass) / passed the test.

4 What would you did / (do) if the teacher (said) / says there was no school tomorrow?

5 If Juan didn't (have to) / had to visit his grandparents, he will / (would) be able to go to the cinema.

2 Compete the sentences.

1 _____ (the weather / good / if / were), I'd go to the beach.

2 If my mum were here, _____ (be / she / angry / would).

3 If we had money, _____ (the / stadium / we / go to / would / football).

4 If the bridge were closed, _____ (would / the / use / tunnel / we).

5 _____ (Miguel / more / studied / if), he'd pass his exams.

3 Complete the sentences with the pairs of action words below. Make any necessary changes and remember to use would.

be/give   be/order   be/practise   do/become   say/discover   win/buy

1 If I _____ in my favourite restaurant at the moment, I _____ a burger and chips!

2 Marta _____ on the school football team if she _____ more.

3 If I _____ the lottery, I _____ a sports car.

4 What _____ (you) if you _____ you had to move to a different city?

5 We _____ very happy if the teacher _____ us no homework for a month!

6 What _____ (he) if he _____ famous?

4   What would you do in the situations below? Write sentences.

1   You meet your favourite athlete.

If I met my favourite athlete, I would be very nervous.

2   You find a lot of money in the park.

_____

3   Your school decides to close one month early for summer.

_____

4   Your best friend gives you a very expensive smartphone.

_____

5   Your parents decide to sell your home and move to a large house in the countryside.

_____

5   Read the magazine article. What is teleportation?

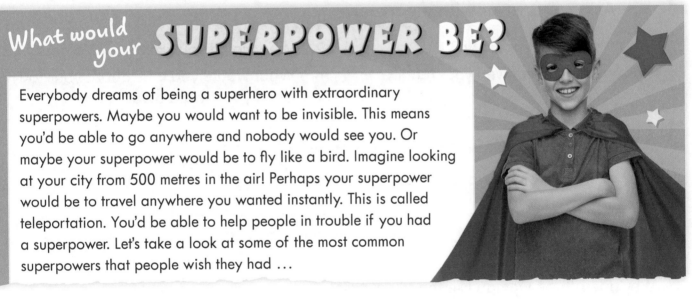

What would your SUPERPOWER BE?

Everybody dreams of being a superhero with extraordinary superpowers. Maybe you would want to be invisible. This means you'd be able to go anywhere and nobody would see you. Or maybe your superpower would be to fly like a bird. Imagine looking at your city from 500 metres in the air! Perhaps your superpower would be to travel anywhere you wanted instantly. This is called teleportation. You'd be able to help people in trouble if you had a superpower. Let's take a look at some of the most common superpowers that people wish they had ...

6   Listen to Ben and Ruth talk about the magazine article in 5. Answer the questions.

1   What would Ben's superpower be?   _____

2   How would he help people who are ill?   _____

3   What would Ruth's superpower be?   _____

4   What would she do if she had this superpower?   _____

7   What would your superpower be? How would you use it? Tell a partner.

I can use the second conditional.

Story lab

READING

I will read a poem.

THE LIFE SWAP

1 Find the words and expressions in *The Life Swap* and write a definition for each one. Use the context of the poem to help you.

1 get me down _____

2 swap places _____

3 shock _____

4 miss _____

2 🗨 Ask and answer with a partner.

1 What things get you down?

2 Who would you like to swap places with?

3 Has anything ever given you a shock?

4 What would you miss about your town/ city if you moved away?

3 Read *The Life Swap* and answer the questions.

1 Why does the woman want to move to the city?

_____

2 Why does the man want to move to a small countryside town?

_____

3 Why doesn't the woman like the city at first?

_____

4 What does the man miss about the city?

_____

5 What does the woman do when she misses her countryside town?

_____

6 How does the man visit the city when he misses it?

_____

4 Read the diary entries again. Write *W* (woman), *M* (man) or *B* (both).

1 This person can live with family if there are any problems in the future. _____

2 This person has been messaging another person. _____

3 This person is going to buy a house. _____

4 This person doesn't want to be late for an important event. _____

5 This person has been dreaming about something for a while. _____

6 This person met someone for the first time. _____

5 Choose either the man or the woman. Write a diary entry for the day before they exchange houses. Think about:

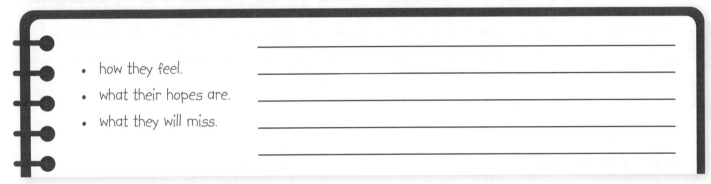

- how they feel.
- what their hopes are.
- what they will miss.

_____

_____

_____

_____

_____

6 Look at the skyscrapers and the key. What is the volume of each one?

MATHS ZONE

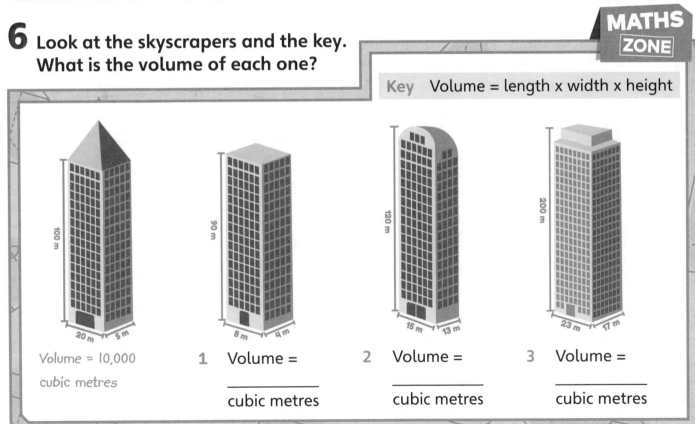

Key Volume = length x width x height

Volume = 10,000 cubic metres

1 Volume = _____ cubic metres

2 Volume = _____ cubic metres

3 Volume = _____ cubic metres

I can read a poem.

Experiment lab

DESIGN: WATER FEATURES

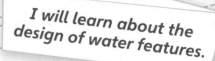

1 **Look and label the water features. Which have you got in your town or city?**

> fountain   pool   water jet   water tunnel   water wall   waterfall

_____   _____   _____   _____   _____   _____

_____   _____   _____   _____   _____   _____

2 **Complete the sentences.**

1   You can find a lot of water features in _____ in cities.

2   We like to see water in a city because it makes a change from _____ and grey.

3   People's behaviour _____ around water features.

4   People love to _____ .

5   Water makes people want to stop and look at it, touch it, _____ it.

6   Children want to play in water because of _____ features.

3 💡 **Read the sets of questions below. Choose one set and go online to find the answers.**

1 How much money is thrown into the Trevi Fountain in Rome, Italy, every day and what happens to it? Why do people in some countries throw coins into water?

2 Where in the world can you find the tallest fountain? How high does the water reach?

3 Where in the world can you find the largest artificial waterfall? How high is it?

4 💬 **Find two students who researched the other sets of questions. Tell them about what you found out.**

5 **Read the blog about recycling water and answer the questions.**

USE WATER
AGAIN AND AGAIN

Hi, welcome to my blog. I'm going to talk about recycling. Hopefully, all of you recycle plastic and paper, but how many of you recycle water? It's a simple and effective way of helping to save the planet. Read on for some useful tips!

1 Use a shower bucket

The next time you have a shower, use a bucket to collect water when you first switch it on. This way, you don't waste the water that's not heated up. You might be surprised how much cold water we waste before a shower gets to a comfortable temperature.

2 Reuse your pasta water

The next time you make spaghetti, don't pour the cooking water away. Let it cool down and use it to water your house plants.

3 Reuse your grey water

What's grey water? This is the dirty water that remains after you have washed your clothes or had a shower. It's ideal to use to flush the toilet or even water plants in your garden. Make sure it contains no harmful chemicals from the detergent or soap, though!

So, there you have it. Recycling water is a very easy thing to do.

1 Why do we normally waste water when we have a shower?

_____

2 How can we recycle water after we have made pasta?

_____

3 What should we do if we want to use grey water in our garden?

_____

Values Choose your environment.

6 💡 **Discuss the questions with a partner.**

1 Why is the water in water features recycled?

2 Do you recycle water? If so, how? If not, will you start to do it?

3 What would happen if there wasn't enough water in the world for everybody?

EXPERIMENT TIME

Report

1 **Think about your experiment. Discuss with a partner.**

- What worked?
- What went wrong?
- What will you do differently next time?

 **I know** about the design of water features.

Go over the bridge, ...

COMMUNICATION: PREPOSITIONS OF MOVEMENT

I will ask for and give directions.

1 Look and match.

1 past   ____
2 around   ____
3 across   ____
4 over   ____
5 through ____
6 along   ____

2 🔊 040 Look at the maps below and listen to the conversation. Tick ☑ the map that is being described.

a ☐

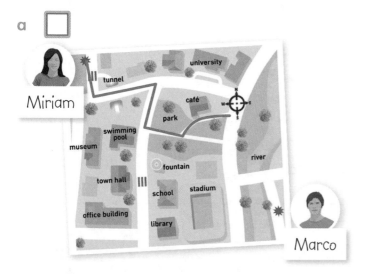

b ☐

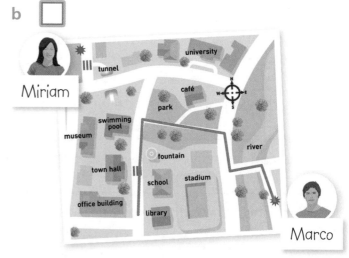

3 💬 Work in pairs and look at the maps in 2. Take turns to describe the following routes.

1 Miriam to the fountain
2 Marco to the office building
3 Miriam to the library
4 Marco to the park

4 💬 Work in pairs. Think of a place near your school. Ask your partner for directions to it from your school.

Excuse me. How do I get to the park?

Go across the road ...

I can ask for and give directions.

Writing lab

WRITING INSTRUCTIONS

I will write instructions in an email.

1 Read and complete.

> across   around   over   past   through

To: Mandy | **Subject:** Finding my house for the party

Hi Mandy,

How is it going? Are you coming to my party on Saturday evening? It's going to be so much fun!

OK, you asked how to find my house. It's really simple. When you get off the bus at the bus station, go **1** _____ the street to the museum. Turn right and go **2** _____ the town hall. You'll then see a bridge. Go **3** _____ the bridge and go across the street to the park. Go **4** _____ the park, **5** _____ the fountain and then leave the park. My house is just opposite. Easy, right?

So, remember the party starts at 6:30 p.m. See you then!

Best,

Olivia

2 Read the email again and answer the questions.

1   What word does Olivia use in her greeting? _____

2   What is the purpose of the first paragraph? _____

3   What is the purpose of the second paragraph? _____

4   What information does Olivia include in her final paragraph?
    _____

5   What word does Olivia use in her closing? _____

3 Write an email to a friend giving them directions to your house. Think about:

- where you are giving directions from
- what greeting you are going to use
- why you are writing to your friend

- the information to include in your final paragraph
- the word you are going to use in your closing

 **I can** write instructions in an email.

Create a project to change your city

Project report

1 💡 Answer the questions. Then discuss with a partner.

1 What city projects did you find for: best water feature project, most innovative project, most ecological project and most modern project?

_____

2 Where did you find out about the best city projects?

_____

3 Why do you think your choices are the best examples in each category?

_____

4 What is your city project?

_____

5 How did you decide what your city project will be?

_____

6 Is there anything like your project in other cities around the world?

_____

7 How will your project improve your city?

_____

2 Complete your project report.

- What did you find easy about your project?
  _____

- What did you find difficult about your project?
  _____

- If you did the project again, what changes would you make?
  _____

- Which other city projects in the class do you find interesting? Why?
  _____

3 💬 Present your city project to your family and friends.

I can create a project to change my city.

1 Unscramble the words and use them to complete the text.

ftnniauo   grdbeis   itamdus   lnnteu   oiecff   ssskycrrpea   tainolirtad   ttsseua

IN MY CITY

There are a lot of things to see and do in my city. That's why I love living here. When you visit my city, you will see a lot of modern buildings, like 1 _____ and 2 _____ buildings, and a lot of 3 _____ buildings. Some of these are more than 200 years old! There is also a huge park, where I hang around with my friends. In the park, there are some 4 _____ of famous people and there is a 5 _____ . People love this because they throw coins into it. If you love sport, we've got a really famous 6 _____ . It's where the best baseball team in the country plays. There is also a really wide river. There are a lot of 7 _____ that go across the river and even a 8 _____ that goes under it! I would really miss my city if I had to leave.

2 What are your three favourite new words from the unit? Write a definition of each one.

1 _____

2 _____

3 _____

3 🗨 Complete the sentences in your own words. Then discuss with a partner.

1 I would be very happy if _____ .

2 My parents would be very angry if _____ .

3 My best friend would be sad if _____ .

4 If there were no school today, _____ .

5 If I suddenly became world-famous, _____ .

4 Write directions from your home to your school. If necessary, use a dictionary to help you.

_____

_____

4 Checkpoint

UNITS 7 AND 8

1  Listen and follow Maya's path.

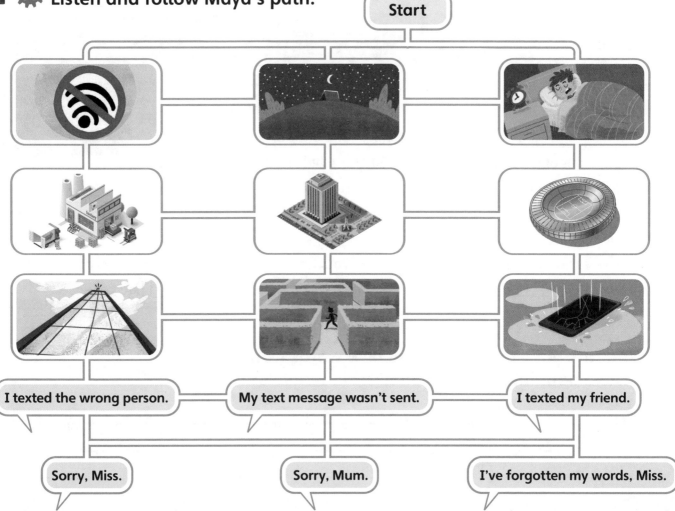

Start

I texted the wrong person.

My text message wasn't sent.

I texted my friend.

Sorry, Miss.

Sorry, Mum.

I've forgotten my words, Miss.

2 Listen again. Complete the sentences with words from Maya's story.

1 **A:** Have you ever _____ in a place?

  B: Yes, when I went to visit my cousin at university, I had to ask for directions.

2 **A:** Does your mother work in the city?

  B: Yes, she's a lawyer. She works in an _____ .

3 **A:** Do you travel across the flyover to get to the airport?

  B: Yes – but you can also drive through a _____ under the river.

4 **A:** Have you ever fallen over in front of people?

  B: Yes. I _____ on some ice on the road once.

5 **A:** What would you do if you were on stage and you _____ your words?

  B: I think I'd just invent something to say.

3 Read the email and draw the route to the university on the map.

NEW MESSAGE　　　**To:** Amir　|　**Subject:** Your visit

Hi Amir!

I'm looking forward to seeing you next week! Here are the directions.

You're coming by train, right? So, to get to the university, come out of the station exit and turn left. Go past the town hall. You can't miss it – there's a big statue opposite it. Go along the street until you reach the canal. Go over the bridge, and turn right. You'll come to a square, with office buildings around it. Go across the square to the other side. My building is on the corner, just next to a water fountain.

If you get lost, just call me.

See you soon!

Shane

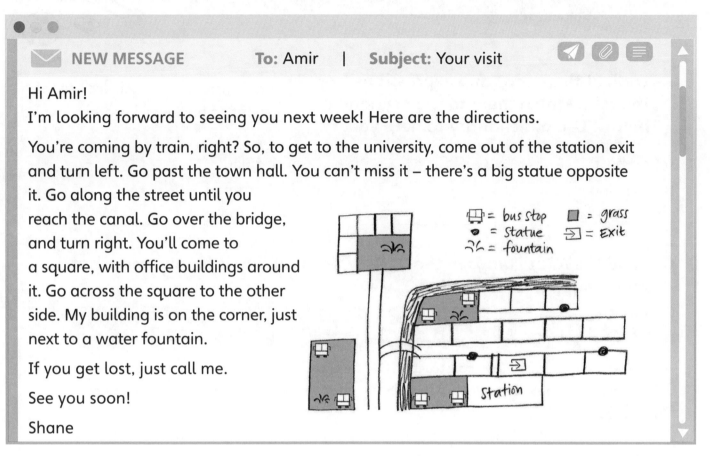

4 Write an email to a friend. Give directions from school to your home.

5 Work in pairs. Read your directions to your partner. Draw a map showing the route you are going to take. Check with your partner. Is the route correct?

How do I get to your house?

Go along Long Street until you get to the bridge. My house is at the end.

The United States of America

CULTURE

1 **Look at the words and expressions from the text. Match them to their synonyms below. Use a dictionary to help you.**

> construction   construct   giant
> go out of business   protect   weird

1   go bust   _____
2   build   _____
3   building   _____
4   strange   _____
5   keep safe   _____
6   very big   _____

2 **Read *Weird buildings in the USA*. Which building is empty and what might happen to it?**

WEIRD BUILDINGS IN THE USA

If you wrote a list of famous constructions in the USA, the Empire State Building in New York City would probably be on it. And then there's the Statue of Liberty, which is found near the Empire State Building.

But would a hotel that looks like a dog or a building that looks like a shopping basket be on your list? These buildings attract many visitors every year, who come to see these weird constructions.

★ ★ DOG BARK PARK INN, COTTONWOOD, IDAHO ★ ★

The state of Idaho is in northwestern USA. It's home to the only hotel in the world that was built in the shape of a giant dog. The Dog Bark Park Inn is found in the small town of Cottonwood and it was created by artist Dennis Sullivan. Dennis was famous for models of dogs that he created out of wood, which were sold in shops. He then decided to make a hotel in the shape of a dog in 1997. Hotel guests can stay in either the head or the stomach of the dog. There are only two rooms, but each one is decorated with dog-shaped furniture.

★ ★ LONGABERGER BASKET BUILDING, NEWARK, OHIO ★ ★

Have you ever seen a building that looks like something you would put your fruit and vegetables in at the greengrocer's? Yes, the Longaberger building in the state of Ohio really does look like a big shopping basket. It was constructed in 1997 as the headquarters of a company called Longaberger, which made shopping baskets. The company went out of business in 2018, and now the building is empty. People were afraid that it would be destroyed, but it is now protected by law.

3 Read again and complete. Use between one and three words.

1 The Empire State Building is in the same _____ as the Statue of Liberty.

2 A lot of people _____ the Dog Bark Park Inn and the Longaberger Basket building every year.

3 Dennis Sullivan used to _____ models of dogs out of wood.

4 If you want to visit the dog hotel, you can sleep in two places: _____ or the stomach.

5 The Longaberger Basket building _____ something you put your shopping in.

6 The Longaberger company _____ exist now.

4 Research and write a description of a weird building in your country. Then present it to the class.

Think about:
- where the building is
- why it is so weird
- who created it
- any other interesting facts about it

I will visit New York and Los Angeles.

5 Plan a trip to the USA and tell a partner about it.

Think about:
- what cities you will visit
- what buildings and monuments you will visit
- what national parks you will visit
- what you will do in the cities and national parks

I know about culture in the USA.

Unit 1

WRITING A NEWS ARTICLE

NEWS ———————————————————— 2ND FEBRUARY

STUDENT FINDS ENVELOPE WITH £5,000 IN LIBRARY BOOK

1 Read the headline. Interview the student and write an article about the news story.

Before you start, make notes about:

- what happened

  [name], a student at a university in ...., had a lucky find during a visit to the library ...

  _____

  _____

- where and when it happened

  [name] was in the library at ...

  _____

- questions to ask the student

  We asked [name] what ...

  _____

- what the student said

  [name] said that ....

  _____

- what happened in the end

  In the end, ...

  _____

Unit 2

WRITING A FACT FILE

1 Write a fact file for a person you think is inspirational. Be sure to include: name, date of birth, place of birth, why they are inspirational and a fun fact.

_____

_____

_____

_____

Unit 3

WRITING A PODCAST FOR AN ADVERTISEMENT

1 Choose a product (it can be real or you can invent one) and write a podcast script to advertise it.

Remember to include:

- questions and exclamations to persuade people to buy the product
- facts about the product
- adjectives and superlative adjectives

2 Interview a famous person and ask them why they like the product.

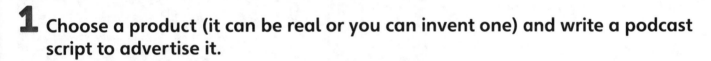

🔊 PODCAST SCRIPT

PRESENTER: Welcome to today's show! We are lucky to have _____ in the studio, to talk about a fantastic new product, _____ . Welcome, _____ !

_____ : Thank you for inviting me to the show!

PRESENTER: Let's talk about the product. What do you like about it?

_____ : _____

PRESENTER: Cool! And is it easy to use?

_____ : _____

_____

_____

Unit 4

1 Read the story below. Think of a suitable title for it.

_____

The door of the spaceship opened and the astronauts looked out at the new planet. Everything was different shades of the colour blue – the ground, the sky, the two Suns, the mountains, the trees and the lake that they could see nearby. Commander Anna McCloud left her spaceship. She took a deep breath and the air was good to breathe. 'It's safe', she said to her team of astronauts, who were following her from the spaceship. Then they heard a loud noise …

2 Continue the story. Think about the things below and also use some of your own ideas.

- What is the name of the new planet?
- Who are the other astronauts?
- What made the loud noise?

- What happens to the astronauts on the new planet?
- What happens at the end of the story?

Unit 5

WRITING A TRAVEL BROCHURE

1 Research and write a travel brochure about a famous or important place.

- Where is it?
- When was it built/discovered?
- Who was it built/discovered/ designed by?
- Why is it famous/important?
- Write two facts about the place and what you can do there.

Unit 6

WRITING A COMIC STRIP STORY

1 Write your own comic strip story. Use the ideas below to help you.

- Who is in your comic strip?
- What happens in your comic strip story?
- What do they say?
- What happens at the end?

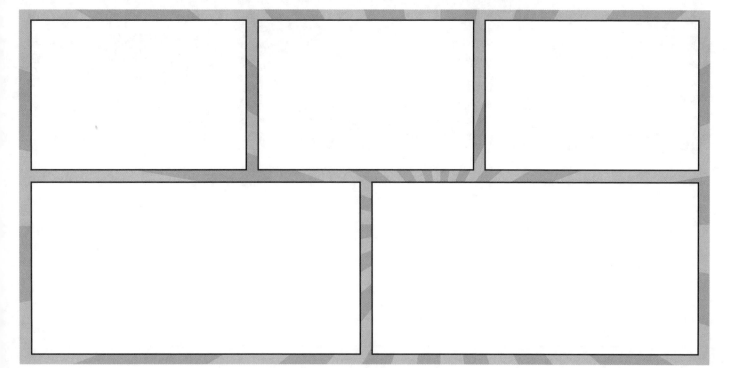

Unit 7

WRITING AN EMAIL

1 **Look at the pictures. You are the boy or the girl in the story. Write an email to your teacher and tell her about what happened!**

Use the question words to help you.

What …?   When …?   Where …?   Who …?   Why …?

How many adjectives and adverbs can you use to say how you felt or how you did things?

Unit 8

WRITING A COMPETITION ENTRY

1 Read about a competition to find the best town or city to live in your country.

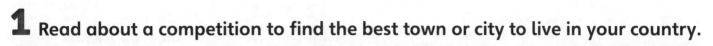

THE BEST PLACE TO LIVE!

Do you think your town or city is the best place to live in the country? Then tell us why. Let us know the name of your town or city and what things you can do there at the weekend. We also want to know what the buildings are like and if there are any interesting water features. The most important thing, however, is to tell us why you think your town or city is the best place to live!

2 Write your competition entry.

_____
_____
_____
_____
_____
_____
_____
_____
_____
_____
_____

Pearson Education Limited
KAO TWO
KAO Park
Hockham Way
Harlow, Essex
CM17 9SR
England
and Associated Companies throughout the world.

english.com/englishcode

First published 2021
Sixth impression 2022

ISBN: 978-1-292-32286-5

Set in Heinemann Roman 12 pt
Printed in Slovakia by Neografia

Argentina

Maria Belen Gonzalez Milbrandt (Director Colegio Sol De Funes), Alejandra Garre (Coordinator Colegio San Patricio), Patricia Bettucci (Teacher Colegio Verbo Encarnado), Colegio Los Arroyos (Coordinator Luciana Pittondo), Instituto Stella Maris (Coordinator Ana Maria Ferrari), Gabriela Dichiara (Coordinator Nivel Pre-Primario En Escuela Normal N° 1 Dr Nicolas Avellaneda), Alejandra Ferreyra & Maria Elena Casals (Profesor Escuela Normal N° 1 Dr Nicolas Avellaneda), Maria Julia Occhi (Primary Director Colegio San Bartolomé Sede Fisherton), Gisele Manzur (English Director- Colegio Educativo Latinoamericano), Griselda Rodriguez (Ex-Directora de Instituto IATEL), Cultural Inglesa de Santa Fe (Olga Poloni y Silvia Cantero), Escuela Primaria de la Universidad Nacional del Litoral (Santa Fe) (Ricardo Noval, Natalia Mártirez y Romina Papini), Colegio La Salle Jobson Santa Fe (Santa Fe) (Miriam Ibañez), Colegio de la Inmaculada Concepción (Santa Fe) (Gabriela Guglielminetti), Colegios Niño Jesús y San Ezequiel Moreno (Santa Fe) (Ivana Serrano), Advice Prep School (Santa Fe) (Virginia Berutti), Centro de Enseñanza de Inglés Mariana G. Puygros (Santa Fe). Focus Group Participants: Alejandra Aguirre (Coordinator Colegio Español), Alicia Ercole (Director Instituto CILEL (Casilda)), Marianella Robledo (Coordinator Insituto CILEL (Casilda)), Viviana Valenti (Director Instituto Let's Go), Natalia Berg (Prof. Colegio de La Paz (San Nicolás)).

Turkey

Ugur Okullari, Isik Okullari, Doğa Koleji, Fenerbahce Koleji, Arı Okullari, Maya Okullari, Yükselen Koleji, Pinar Koleji, Yeşilköy Okullari, Final Okullari, Vizyon Koleji

Image Credits:

123RF.com: apoplexia 56, Buppha Wuttifery 50, Cathy Yeulet 46, cokemomo 62, David Castillo Dominici 86, Eric Isselee 55, georgejmclittle 94, kasza 37, Kostic Dusan 51, Marian Vejcik 8, Nicola Colombo 56, noravector 47, Prima Anandatya Nusantara 41, Scott Rothstein 66, serezniy 24, tele52 118, 118, vchalup 105; **Getty Images:** Adobest 68, 90, Alejandro Jimenez Garrido 51, Alistair Berg 22, CatLane 38, Design Pics / Con Tanasiuk 18, DNY59 112, epicurean 80, EyeEm 51, Fudio 62, Heritage Images 90, John Henley 52, kwanchaichaiudom 62, londoneye 108, matthewleesdixon 51, ntdanai 68, Pierre Leclezio / EyeEm 112, SDI Productions 38, SeanPavonePhoto 112, ugurhan 78; **Pearson Education Asia Ltd:** Coleman Yuen 112; **Pearson Education Ltd:** Jon Barlow 6, 8, 13, 18, 21, 25, 30, 37, 41, 46, 61, 63, 81, 86, 89, 93, 95, 96, 97, 99, 100, 114, 119, 121, Martin Sanders / Beehive Illustration 84; **Shutterstock.com:** 34, Africa Studio 34, 38, 38, 101, agap 75, Alexander Trinitatov 33, AlexAnton 74, AlexeiLogvinovich 51, Alizada Studios 112, andregric 29, Andrey_Popov 94, Birdiegal 55, Bogdan Wankowicz 51, Brina L. Bunt 56, Chaiwuth Wichitdho 47, ChameleonsEye 38, Christopher Elwell 50, costall 55, David Tadevosian 38, Deborah Kolb 53, easyshutter 56, elbud 121, Eric Isselee 50, 56, Evan Lorne 51, Everett Historical 36, FamVeld 30, Frontpage 117, GagliardiImages 31, gangoo 34, garanga 91, Ger Bosma Photos 55, Happetr 94, Happy Together 46, Jeanette Teare 107, Jiang Hongyan 50, Leonid Andronov 91, Liv Oeian 25, lowpower225 112, Lucky Business 94, Lukas Gojda 2, Martyn Skorkin 120, moshimochi 105, mosista 65, Nelli Syrotynska 105, notbad 41, Pakhnyushchy 56, Patric Froidevaux 56, Poznyakov 115, Rastkobelic 64, Rob Marmion 46, RTimages 21, sculpies 90, Simon Poon 51, Skowronek 92, skyhawk x 36, solarseven 64, Stephen Farhall 29, Syda Productions 109, Tero Vesalainen 35, Tyler Olson 105, Valentyn Volkov 29, Victor Habbick 58, Vita Khorzhevska 56, Volodymyr Horbovyy 118, Westend61 27, ZouZou 64

Illustrated by:

Barry Ablett/Beehive Illustration, pp. 57, 72 (top, middle), 85; Julia Castaño/Bright Agency, p.3; Jean Claude/Advocate Art, p.14; Chloe Dijon/Advocate Art, p.54 (bottom); Federica Frenna/Bright Agency, p.9; Alex Hoskins/Lemonade Illustration Agency, pp.13, 18, 41 (2,3,4), 69, 79, 99, 126; Daniel Limon/Beehive Illustration, pp.12, 15, 17, 29, 44 (left), 66, 71 (bottom), 100, 102, 118, 124; Irene Montano/Advocate Art, pp.42, 43; Isabel Muñoz/Bright Agency, pp.7 (left), 63, 70, 80; Milli-Jane Pooley/Lemonade Illustration Agency, pp.16, 38, 44 (right), 54 (top), 72 (bottom), 111, 114 (top); Pedro Riquelme/Advocate Art, p.98; Martin Sanders/Beehive Illustration, pp.10, 40, 41 (1,5,6), 106, 114 (bottom); Kate Sheppard/Beehive Illustration, pp.7 (right), 71 (top), 97, 119; Wendy Tan Shiau Wei/Astound US, p.110; Erin Taylor/Bright Agency, p.82; Sara Ugolotti/Advocate Art, p.26; Joseph Wilkins/Beehive Illustration, pp.4-5.

Cover Image: Front: **Pearson Education Ltd:** Jon Barlow

★ You did it! ★

★ ★ ★ Congratulations! ★ ★ ★